SEVERO SARDUY

FOOTWORK: SELECTED POEMS

SEVERO SARDUY

FOOTWORK: SELECTED POEMS

translated from Spanish by

DAVID FRANCIS

ISBN 978-1-949918-02-1
First edition.

© Severo Sarduy and Heirs of Severo Sarduy 1974–2007.

Selections from first publications:
Big bang: © 1974
Un testigo fugaz y disfrazado: © 1985
Un testigo perenne y delatado: © 1993
Últimos poemas: © 2007, first published 1999

English translation © 2021 David Francis.
All rights reserved.

No part of this publication may be reproduced or transmitted in any form or by any means, electronic or mechanical, including photocopying, recording, or any information storage or retrieval system, without permission in writing from the publisher.

Published by:
Circumference Books
85 East End Avenue #14F
New York, New York 10028
www.circumferencebooks.com

Distributed by:
Small Press Distribution (SPD)
1341 Seventh Street
Berkeley, California 94710-1409
www.spdbooks.org

Printed by  kopa.eu

Contents

Translator's Note   1

Big Bang (1974)   20

Flamenco   22

"Stucco polygons" 24
"The pages covered in gold letters" 26
"Water weds to windows" 28
"The piercing chorus" 30
"white walls" 32
"LIKE A BLACK STONE" 34
Fandangos 36
Tientos 40
Sevillanas 42
Tanguillo 44
Seguidillas 46
Alegrías 48
Zapateado 50
Farruca 52
Mineras 56
Bulerías 60

Mood Indigo   62

Magenta Haze 64
The Mooche 66
Blue Reverie 68
Sophisticated Lady 70
Moon Mist 72
Echoes of Harlem 74
Golden Feathers 76
Tonk 78
Black Spiral 80

Big Bang 82

    I. Big Bang 84
    II. Big Bang 84
    III. Isomorphism 86
    IV. Black Hole 88
    V. Crab 90
    VI. Fossilized Light 92
    XII. Heavenly Body 94

Other Poems 96

    Havana Sextet 98
    Blank Pages (Paintings by Franz Kline) 104
    Carlo Crivelli's Peacock 110
    Cubes by Larry Bell 112
    Inter Femora 114

A Fleeting and Masked Witness
Un testigo fugaz y disfrazado (1985)   **116**

    "The transparent light at midday" 118
    "The murmur of machines was growing" 120
    "Not the voice preceded by the echo" 122
    "Pull out of me more than what was left out" 124
    "Entering you, head to head" 126
    "Glittering, greased, the piston" 128
    "Though you anointed the threshold" 130
    "If it darkened, if it abandoned me" 132
    "Let go, I know this well" 134
    "Not the footstep of the god, but the footprint" 136
    "The humid balconies overlooked" 138
    Page from a Diary 140
    "Now death has taken everything" 142
    "Vanquished, the Powerful One flees" 144
    Requesting the Canonization of Virgilio Piñera 146
    To the Buddha of Chinatown 148
    "Not by chance, for love of nonsense" 150

Morandi 152
Rothko. 154

A Perennial and Betrayed Witness
Un testigo perenne y delatado (1993)   **156**

Sonnets   *158*

    Saint John of the Cross. 160
    Saint Teresa of Ávila 162
    Clarity 164
    Allegory by Holbein. 166
    For the Tree of "La Recoleta" 168
    Ornithomancy. 170
    "What night says to day" 172
    "Red spilled over purple" 174
    "Matta draws the invisible" 176
    "Acrostic traitor: you don't restore". 178
    May the Infinite be Starless 180
    "You put a lace skirt on Medea" 182
    To the Home of the Counts of Jaruco. 184
    Recounting 186
    Portrait. 188
    "More than the dream, the accuracy" 190

Décimas   *192*

    A Crown of Fruits. 194
        I. Cherimoya. 194
        II. Mango 194
        III. Star Apple. 196
        IV. Pineapple 196
        V. Papaya. 198
        VI. Cashew 198
        VII. Loquat. 200
        VIII. Guanábana 200
        IX. Mamey. 202
        X. Colophon 202

In Summer's Amber
    Orishas 204
        I. Olofi, Olodumare, Olorun 204
       II. Elegua 204
     III. Obatala 206
     IV. Shango 206
      V. Oshun 208
     VI. The Ibejis 208
    VII. Oya 210
   VIII. Babalú-Ayé 210
     IX. Olokun 212
      X. Yemoja 212

    Other *Décimas*
      From Phrases Spoken in Spanish by F. W. 214
      "I convince the more I deceive" 216
      "This is what you are, time of grieving" 218

Last Poems/Últimos poemas (1999)   **220**

One   *222*
  "Enemy identical face" 224
  "The gold in *The Count of Orgaz*" 226
  Imitation of a Sonnet 228
  To the Letters of the Alphabet 232

Two   *236*
  Imitation 238

Three   *244*
  Epitaphs 246

Biographies   **254**

Translator's Note

> I do not remember love, only desire;
> not the lack of faith, only the sphere —
> the image facing its reflection
>
> with white texture, the true
> page — or your body, which I still reread —:
> vast ideogram of spring.
>
> —Severo Sarduy

Beginnings

THE SCARRED BODY OR THE IMAGE OF ITS ABSENCE? Faced with the question of how to translate the "body" of Severo Sarduy's poetry, I feel a sense of stuttering: how to convey the enormity of seeming contradiction I encountered while translating his poems, indeed a body of work that sings on its own, that celebrates the carnal life, the sensual experiences of dance, of painting, food, music, and sexual pleasure, but that also recognizes — in these pleasures — the imminence of one's passing? In his 56 years of life, the exiled poet, novelist, essayist, painter, and world traveler managed to include such a vast range of perspectives in his texts that to discuss him and his writing also means to risk an all-too-simple presentation of his brilliant work.

Severo Sarduy was not known to follow convention. Nor did he think that conventional approaches to storytelling or lyrical composition could capture the complexities of human behavior or personal and national identity. His groundbreaking contributions to the writing of (a) Latin American, or national, character or literary histories were not happenstance, as the publication of his major works followed the Cuban Revolution and the political turmoil that would ensue with Castro's rise and Cuban dictator Fulgencio Batista's loss of power in 1958. As Boom literature — galvanized by such authors as Mario Vargas Llosa, Julio Cortázar, and Carlos Fuentes — brought Latin America increasing visibility on the world literary stage, this gay author and artist, son of a railroad worker, redefined Latin American approaches to the writing of literature from the vantage point of his exile in France and from many other parts of the world he visited after departing his country of birth.

Born in 1937 in Camagüey, Cuba, Sarduy started writing at an early age, publishing in his teenage years in various Cuban literary magazines between Camagüey and Havana. After pursuing studies in medicine in Cuba's capital, he left the island on a scholarship in 1960 to study art criticism in Europe, traveling to Madrid and then to Paris. Aware of Fidel Castro's efforts to police homosexuality and "reeducate" gay men in work camps called Military Units to Aid Production (UMAP), the writer would reside for the rest of his life in Paris, never to return home.

Sarduy achieved considerable notoriety before his life was cut short in 1993 due to complications with AIDS. The author's first novel, *Gestos* ("Gestures"), was published in 1963, but the book by which he is most recognized is *De donde son los cantantes* (1967), an experimental work of fiction that Suzanne Jill Levine translated deftly into English as *From Cuba with a Song* in 1972. Internationally celebrated for his work, Sarduy won France's prestigious Medici Prize for his novel *Cobra* (1972). Indeed, critics published extensively on the author's novels and essays and continue to write about his poetry.

Sarduy's works contain an often chaotic convergence of linguistic registers and characters, whose bodies—dressed in drag, tattooed, or scarred—distort, reconfigure, or "explode" (in Big Bang fashion or in little deaths) bourgeois efforts to codify or define a singular Latin American identity.[1] The author's texts incorporate such a variety of voices from within and beyond Cuba that Richard Howard hailed Sarduy as a writer who "has everything...so brilliant, so funny, and so bewilderingly apt in his borrowings, his derivations, as well as in his inventions;"[2] for his part, Gabriel García Márquez once called Sarduy the best writer in the Spanish language.[3] Acknowledging the significant amount of praise for Sarduy's life and literature, in what ensues I write about the life of his poetry and my process of translating it. In doing so, my hope is to invite new audiences to, and interpretations of, his remarkable, and living, lyrical corpus.

Lyrical Encounteers

With so much attention already given to Sarduy's writing, one may wonder why no collection of his poems, prior to this work, has been published in English. The multiplicity of vocabularies, tones, registers, and perspectives that so intrigued Sarduy and that he condenses into his poetry make his writing impossible to translate in any one way that encompasses the various interpretations that his original texts offer. Nevertheless, when I first encountered Sarduy's sonnets in the stacks of the University of Virginia's Alderman Library in the spring of 2009, I did not see the difficulty of translating the poet's lines as an impediment to translation's process, but rather as an appeal to deep reading and connection. At the time, I was preparing for my MA exams in Spanish. I was also coming to terms with my own sexuality and struggling to find the language to speak about it. And then I found Sarduy's *Daiquirí* (1980), a tiny collection of eight sonnets later republished in *Un testigo fugaz y disfrazado* (*A Fleeting and Masked Witness*) in 1985. To print only eight poems in, and as, a collection was, to me, a claim unto itself, that brevity when writing on sex and queer desire might be sufficient, or even a provocation. With each sonnet, the miniature book enraptured me, encapsulating a music that sung unabashedly about longing and how complicated, and celebrated, an intimate encounter might be. Without landing on any singular statement of truth, the obstacles of articulating the memory of ecstasy or the image of an absent beloved became opportunities to embrace the difficulties of reading and writing *through* another writer's lyrical compositions. I found myself obsessed with the collection's complexities, its seemingly cosmic erudition, its joy in double entendre, and its resistance to any one sort of interpretation. That same spring, I shared Sarduy's sonnets in a course on translation, led by one of Sarduy's friends and correspondents, Gustavo Pellón. Through that class, translation became an act of shared readership, where classmates debated word choices that would have significant bearing on the way a line might rhyme or convey meaning. While dialogue with the author was not possible and language about sexuality faltered (for me) beyond the page, dialogue with readers of poetry—in Spanish and English—gave me an opening to think about the richness of difficulty—of desire, of difference, and of the certainty of death, not as foreclosure but as movement toward speech—as both voice and silence.

Faith to Form: Sarduy's (Neo-)Baroque Contradictions

Reading Sarduy's verse since I first encountered it has further elucidated the complexities of the poet's imaginative textual structures and the pleasures of translating beyond his novels' forms. His poems are deceptive, ludic, often erotic, and they offer multiple contradictory narratives that make their sense more meaningful in contradiction. To be sure, this is an effect of the Neo-Baroque aesthetic Sarduy enlivens in his verse. The author's play with lyrical form, sound, rhyme, rhythm, meter, inverted and unusual syntax, high- and low- register vocabularies, and neologisms mask and unmask the multiplicity of manners by which a line or even a word might be translated. Beyond the poems' content, a mathematical rigor contains the syllabic structures of much of his verse, a rigor that requires a level of rule-breaking in English in order to rewrite a poem's music in English while also conveying the original text's message. To that point, the Spanish sonnets' hendecasyllabic lines are not governed by the same numerical strictness in English. Nevertheless, sometimes Sarduy's measured incantations are so tightly interwoven with a poem's form that to modify them would be to lose much of their acoustic delight. Note, for instance, the fricative consonants "s" and "z" that end each line in "The gold in *The Count of Orgaz*" (in both languages) or the author's brilliant abecedarian, "To the Letters of the Alphabet," written on 8-8-88. In the latter poem, the first and last letter of each line follow the letters of the Spanish alphabet. Not only is remaining "faithful" to such a precise form challenging, but it can also be fun. It requires an element of play with words, as if they were puzzle pieces on a page framed by the alphabet's sequential chain. Translating a Spanish-alphabet poem into English meant also that, at least for this poem, as the translator, I could place into the English alphabet the visualization of the Spanish phoneme we hear at the beginning of the line, "llano filled, combined, in the words of Lull." It also meant that the concept of a letter in Spanish ("ll") required a different sort of attention in English, where the new English alphabet, according to Sarduy's translated poem, might now contain 27 letters.

The relationship between faithfulness to form and the verbal play articulated within form comes alive in the process of translating Sarduy. But to understand how to translate Sarduy's forms, I have also wanted to study Sarduy's seemingly coterminous desire to break with tradition. Reading his earlier poems, one observes that Sarduy's so-called "surface of the text,"[4] the manner in which each word is positioned around the page's white space, often functions as a (mis)leading metric by which to interpret the poem's depth, its content. Poems from *Flamenco* (1969) or *Mood Indigo* (1970) make this point. Contextualized in Sarduy's readings of spatial cosmologies, "[LIKE A BLACK STONE]" guides—graphically—the eye's elliptical movement around the text's white space and leads the viewer's eyes to follow the comparable pathways of planetary orbits around the sun, creating the outline of a misshapen circle—a modified form, of sorts—about which Johannes Kepler wrote in the 17th-century. The poem also reflects the eye's contours, fabricating the sensation that, as with a mirror image on water, one cannot look *beyond* the text's surface; rather, the text reflects the eye of the spectator. Lacking language, the interior image of the eye—the elliptical white space on the page or the idea of the reader's interpretive eye—is a void around which words circulate. The risk in reading this poem only as a formal rendering, however, is to see its meaning only in the image it makes on the page and not, also, in its words' music. To avoid missing meaning within the language of the poem, I decided to cut the lines in pieces, to read them as prose and in opposing directions, from right to left on the page, from bottom to top. Hearing the lines out loud, one perceives their music. In the Spanish, for instance, the line "SOBRE UNA PIEDRA BLANCA" creates assonant rhyme with the line "TAPANDO UNA VENTANA." Though I could not recreate a comparable rhyme in the same lines in English, I wrote slant rhymes elsewhere, where the content of the lines also calls, I believe, for music: for example, between the lines "the gardens' indigo" and "the echoing patios." From the beginning, such echoes in sound belie in Sarduy's work a body of music often masked by the shapes of his texts.

At times, Sarduy's poems allude to Spain's colonial past and Spanish colonial letters. Even when they do not, they often reinvigorate a Spanish 17th-century Baroque aesthetic in the writer's vision of the past, thereby accumulating vast perspectives and ways of containing or intimating lost history. In the work of translating music into the English versions of Sarduy's poems, my aim was to learn also about the relationships between musical style and repetition in Spanish. But, in the process of doing so, repetition within the Spanish language became as much about syntax and rhythm as it was about the histories that Sarduy's texts could *not* contain. In "Mood Indigo," for instance, leaps between words on the page magnify a broken narrative of departures and arrivals, geographically and temporally, between the violence of the Atlantic slave trade and the composition of jazz music in the 20th century. Following Duke Ellington's eponymous song, the poem, according to J. Edgar Bauer, exemplifies, both in form and content, locations "from which or to which a significant displacement of Black history has taken place."[5] Departures from traditional narrative or lyrical structures underline as much as they elucidate the significance of dislocations from an origin or a linguistic meaning. Such narrative aberrations gain visibility as one observes the absence of words on a page. Bauer and others have written about these concerns in the context of Sarduy's Spanish, African, and Chinese heritage, intrinsically intertwined with the island's history of slavery and indentured labor. While translating "[LIKE A BLACK STONE]" too, it became evident that the process of re-articulating the text's proper nouns was founded in the specificity of terms recognizable beyond a single language. At the same time, I saw the poem's rhythm translated in its repeated iterations of the words "from" and "to."

Why "Footwork"?

Finding a title for this collection—a title that might encapsulate the breadth of Sarduy's literary concerns and motifs—presented its own set of challenges. In considering Sarduy's own beginnings in a world beyond Cuba, I cannot help but think of his first arrival in Spain and wonder how his time there impacted *Flamenco*. The title of this collection of translations, therefore, honors that earlier publication and is derived, also, from the distances Sarduy and his poems would subsequently travel. The word "footwork" also recognizes how Sarduy's poems deliver devastating wit, which lands on its prototypical feet or adroitly maneuvers, purposefully, around naming objects, people, or body parts and toward unexpected endings. The poems' frequent allusions to rhythm and movement further ground for me Sarduy's interests in the relationships between body and form, song and verbal expression. *Flamenco* makes these relationships clear in its poems' titles, each representative of a style of a flamenco dance. Indeed, the title of one poem, "Zapateado," may be translated as "tap dance" or, more to the point, the stomping of feet (the verb "zapatear" comes from the noun "zapato," for shoe). However, the term, like others that Sarduy utilizes, cannot be completely translated and may be traced historically to a form of flamenco dance in Andalusia, in the southern region of Spain, a form whose style of quick heal- and toe- stomping had traveled to Cuba and across the Americas long before Sarduy first alighted in Spain. The curious reader might take a glance, for instance, at the *Álbum pintoresco de la isla de Cuba* ("Picturesque Album of the Island of Cuba"), which dates from the 1850s and whose graphic representations of island life there include a representation of a man and woman dancing the *zapateado* in a rural landscape. Migrations of musical style and structure, which bring with them their own forms of revision and geographic re-contextualization, cannot be detangled from understandings of Sarduy's poetics regarding how the body or a concept, within each poem, moves and may be described or intimated in song. Nor can a historical appreciation of Sarduy's early life in Cuba—his time living outside of the capital city (in Camagüey), the Cuban Revolution, and his exposure to leading Cuban writers like José Lezama Lima—be separated from the primary language in which he chose to write for the rest of his life.

Frequently, Sarduy's verbal and temporal congeries are deeply transgressive or (homo)erotic, sometimes explicitly so, sometimes not. While translating these moments, however, I have developed greater appreciation for the rhetorical movements that bring the reader to them. In Sarduy's *Big Bang* (published first in 1973 and then in 1974, to include *Flamenco* and *Mood Indigo*), movement in time and perspective takes place in the narratives' apparently celestial and even cerebrally scientific fields—descriptive of a "swelling" or "expanding" universe—and then the vantage point quickly shifts. See, for instance, "Black Hole," in which Sarduy's text paints the image of, "the deformation of space around a massive body [which] is compared to a horizontal rubber membrane beneath the weight of a ball." Similar shifts in perspective occur in "Isomorphism," where the speaker begins describing an astrophysics conference in Texas and ends homing in on the interior landscape of a bedroom:

> *You break against the ground small pitchers of spoiled water, you take out your sex, smelling of olives, squeeze your gland, marking it with your fingers stained with saffron, with purple dye.*
> *Milk on the wall: thick point, white sign dilating.*
> *Silence.*
> *Laughter.*

The dilated chasms or negative spaces to which Sarduy's poems refer, rather than bringing to light a traditional ideological point or moral, create a figure around which to comprehend a body's gestures. Translating Sarduy's poems is also a gesture toward verbal transport and requires research on celestial terminologies and a faithfulness to formal "dilations" on the page. In some of Sarduy's poems, distances and time traveled are not merely global, but also simultaneously cosmic and deeply intimate. In other poems, knowledge of and proximity to the unnamed beloved might be subsumed or merely alluded to with paradoxically pointed and haunting ambiguity. By formally depicting heavenly or corporal contractions on the page, Sarduy's poetic works, already in the 1970s, function to illustrate—indeed, to call into question—the reader's capacity to search or read back for an origin of time, for a complete history, or for an unfragmented understanding of that self which yearns, still, for contact with, and understanding of, another. It should not go unnoticed that such a repeated gesture betrays also an obsession with "recuperating" that which has been forever lost, which, as Roberto González Echevarría argues, is Cuba.[6]

Translating Sex, Specificity, and Idiom

Similar to his earlier poems, Sarduy's sonnets in *A Fleeting and Masked Witness* (1985) are interlaced occasionally with different languages, as with the French term, "*hyalo-miel*," a honied gel, mentioned in "If it darkened, if it abandoned me" and referring to lubricant. The sonnets also sometimes incorporate Cuban idiomatic phrases. Such shifts in register, tone, and language make the task of the translator ever more complex. The use of a French proper noun in "If it darkened," for instance, suggests the specificity of experience for one who thinks in one language but who has traveled outside the limitations of that one language's linguistic and cultural sphere. The term *hyalo-miel*'s use, rendered in my translation of the poem as "honey," however, is not simply a consequence of travel, but also of the encounter of a specific foreign object, which (at least for the fictional character of the poem) the speaker sees, acquires, incorporates into his (or her) vocabulary, and applies to the physical body during intercourse. In light of the poem's content, which imagines the possibility of a sexual encounter that fails to achieve penetration (despite attempts to the contrary), the result of such an exchange of terms is ironic. Although the product's purpose is to act as a bridge between two bodies, to lubricate, to minimize friction, to "make [a] slippery" connection, to facilitate, in other words, the penetration of one body into the other, the act of intercourse and its failure are visualized simultaneously, and perhaps more successfully, within and by the interlacing of tongues.[7] Following the identification and procurement of *hyalo-miel*, the speaker's language in the original Spanish text is marked by such an instance of linguistic commerce: between the Spanish-language speaker of the poem and the experience that called for the object's purchase and subsequent use. The unfortunate event after such a purchase is that despite the lubricant's function—to facilitate an interconnection and intimate link between lovers—the moment described results in "blows," in, according to the speaker, a physical disconnect between one lover's failed objective and the other's shared desire. Although I debated keeping the French term *hyalo-miel* in the English translation, I decided, ultimately, that the musical tones evoked with the juxtaposition of French and English words were more disruptive to an English-language translation than in the original Spanish poem. And while the sentiment of failure might still be evoked without the French term, "miel," in French, as in Spanish, indeed, means honey.

Impressively, Sarduy's poem paints a private scene by alluding also to a well-known verse by the Peruvian writer César Vallejo ("The Black Heralds"), whose "blows in life" lead to the speaker's proclamation, simply, that "I do not know." While Vallejo's poem is not erotic, Sarduy's intertextual excesses in verbiage spill beyond a single language. They amplify *how* linguistic overflow—a central element of the (Neo-)Baroque—discloses a distance between intimate subjects whose longing for each other cannot be fulfilled by using a product or the encounter of innovative, privately disclosed diction. But "do not blame 'it'," the poem instructs us, and we are reminded of the value not of proper nouns, or of propriety, but of destabilizing humor. The poem instructs its reader to view botched attempts at connection with levity in the light of our mortality, in light of how even the subject of desire—"it"—is never named, but rather occluded, also, in language. Failure in delivery is a part of life and a part of death, and my hope is that the reader sees continued opportunities for linguistic play with nouns and phrases that, at first glance, deflect immediate recognition in the poems' English translations.

Death and Translation

Publishing Sarduy's poems in translation, the end of the process of translating these works, brings with it a sort of little death. Likewise, in the process of revising the poems, I find in them a sense of liveliness, the notion that, although no collection of terms in English will mirror exactly the effects of Sarduy's poems in Spanish, the translations find new life in the ongoing work of articulating them differently. At the same time, I feel a sense of loss in not being able to share with the author my interpretations of his verse and continued questions I have for him about his poems, some of which remain to be translated. Throughout his life, long before he contracted HIV, Sarduy's writing evinced a consciousness of absence through mortality. On Sarduy's collection of essays, *Barroco* (1974), González Echevarría writes that the work

> makes a formal effort to integrate the annihilation of the subject in the process that constitutes the essay itself: the opening of the book, which follows a numerical scheme, is a zero, the "echo chamber." That "echo chamber" is the authorial I at the beginning of writing: its essence is absence, whiteness encircled by the blackness of the graphic figure—whiteness of the beginning, of snow, of cocaine that expands consciousness—the invisible wall from which voice bounces back as voices: the whiteness of death. White means death in Afro-Cuban cosmology.[8]

Given his interests in Buddhist thought, I am not surprised that Sarduy's poetic works also focus, so often, on the annihilation of the subject. Following Sarduy's shape poems, the empty space, framed in the shape of a zero, is voiced also in Sarduy's more traditional forms:

> Pull out of me more than what was left out:
> for when reaching and defining aporia
> a planet on the other side of its day
> ignites in the night of its senses.
>
> Not by force: for the humid temple
> (of Venus, the second) does not take pleasure
> in being wounded by the Berninian arrow
> or by frenzy. Someday you will lay
>
> lubricants or natural substances
> between the borders with cunning
> prudence, or with salivated caution
>
> that might ease the burning of your entrance:
> because with love and with ardor in the annals
> of history our nuptials are ciphered.

So explicitly erotic in its opening line, Sarduy's sonnet begins with instructions on the writing and reading of the speaker's past, as if it were a physical, intimate endeavor: "pull out of me more than what was left out." The Spanish version "omítemela más" is, perhaps, subtler in its innuendo, and it is multifarious in the possibility of its signification. The verb with which the poem begins—*omitir*—means "to omit" or "to keep from," but the feminine pronoun "la"—that which is to be omitted from the speaker—is never directly named. One might imagine "it" may refer either to the male member, which may also be alluded to with the feminine pronoun in the Spanish language. However, "it" may also be history, "la historia," referred to in the sonnet's final stanza.

As with most poems, before determining how the first line might be interpreted, listening to the poem read out loud can be instructive. "Omítemela más" sounds similar to its opposite command, "O, métemela más," translated roughly as, "oh, enter me more." The verb *meter* means "to put in" while the instruction "*métemela*" is a common cliché in bed. The first line's articulation of the words "o, meter" as *omitir*, nevertheless, is an inversion of the common phrase. And while the choice of the verb *omitir* indicates the possibility of considering one verbal command and its opposite, no similar phrase in English allows for such a play on words whose sounds, while partially akin to each other, oppose each other in meaning. The potential for a confused reading of (or listening to) the Spanish is articulated more directly in the second line's philosophy, encapsulated in the term "aporia," which, by definition, derives from the Greek ἀπορία, conveying a sense of doubt or confusion and, in its Greek roots (*a + poros*), a lack of passage.[9] In its Spanish definition, the term also haracterizes the first line's command in that it is, "a declaration that expresses or contains an impracticality of rational order."[10] In both the Spanish and the English, as with "If it darkened," Sarduy's poem is masterfully, physically erotic and, at the same time, cerebral, distanced. Calling for more omission of that which has already been omitted is a call to negate something already negated. It is an expressed double negative that both resists interpretation and invites further analysis. Whereas later lines in the poem reveal an eventual "entrance" (in history or the body) and the possibility of depth beyond omission. It is precisely this initial beckoning call for omission and deferral that leads to the speaker's philosophical conclusion (and the reader's continued reading). Omission ends, in other words, with the same speaker's imagined union with the other: their shared "nuptials"—are "ciphered" "*in* the annals / of history," and they are done so "with love and with ardor." With the phallic figure of the "Berninian arrow" followed by the term "annals," Sarduy's sonnet is hinting, not so subtly now, at the coveted, and consequently not yet enacted or seen, configurations of anal sex. Considering a poem that stages such carnal and cerebral sentiments, often foreclosed or quieted in a predominantly heterosexual literary landscape, any gay author publishing sonnets in the 1980s may have wondered whether their works would have "entered" the annals of (literary) history. For these reasons, as translator, I hope that later readers of the poem in English will find new ways to interpret its opening line. In the end, I have opted for a more explicit translation in "pull out of me more," given also the subsequent more philosophical terms that indicate a failed (writerly or physical) passage.

With this in mind, I would emphasize, too, that the poem's final word—"ciphered"—serves as an explanation for the possibility of interpreting the (or a) poem in multiple ways. Lest one read in the sonnet a singular vision of hope for the memory of the poem's lovers, the text encapsulates history's paradox in which hidden or omitted love is alluded to in code and therefore blots out the lovers' memory. Additionally, at least in Spanish, the poem begins and ends in zero: first, with the letter "o" in the verb "omítemela," and, last, in the etymology of the final word. "Ciphered" ("*cifrada*," in Spanish), derives "from Arabic *sifr* [صفر] 'zero,' literally 'empty, nothing.'"[11] The sonnet's vocabulary indicates, however, that there is no single key or code necessary to gain initial access to the poem or others. To *be* ciphered is to imply a later and welcome action of interpretation, to be *de*ciphered; and in this relationship between reader and text lies the reciprocal act of reading as translation, as an act of entrance and extraction, of reading and re-writing.

Mysticism, Renunciation, and Dance

> The crisis of engulfment can come from a wound, but also from a fusion: we die together from loving each other: an open death, by dilution into the ether, a closed death of the shared grave.
>
> —Roland Barthes, *A Lover's Discourse*

One may wonder how the act of deciphering Sarduy's texts might be understood for a translator also interested in conveying, to the extent possible, what the poems do structurally in the original Spanish. How might the processes of reading and (re-)writing—interpreting and translating—be aligned for Sarduy's Neo-Baroque? Near the end of his life, in a 1992 essay entitled "Bosquejo para una lectura erótica del *Cántico espiritual* seguido de *Imitación*" ("Outline for an erotic reading of the *Spiritual Canticle* followed by *Imitation*"), Sarduy discusses a poem by the mystical poet Saint John of the Cross, providing several approaches to interpreting the 16th-century mystic's work. At the essay's conclusion, however, Sarduy urges imitation, rather than interpretation, as a form of readerly reflection. For this final approach to interpreting the saint's poetry, he writes:

The other possible approach, by definition blasphemous or infatuated, is that of freeing oneself to imitation. Mimesis instead of reading; double and simulacrum instead of interpretation. Reflection, forcibly deformed, the divine epithalamium. To go in the copy toward the materialization of metaphors, clearly mark out the ellipses, go down the road one more time: from the body in flame to God, from desire to fusion with the One....[12]

Sarduy then shares his own poem, "Imitation," containing the following stanzas:

> I was living in peace;
> my body has become exiled from itself,
> and gains pleasure still
> from that which, hushed,
> you gave it at night, running over.
>
> More than wine, the nectar I relished
> from your cellar made me drunk,
> now I've lost touch and caution,
> now nothing soothes me,
> but for the spill that shines and blinds.

For readers familiar with Spanish mystical poetry, "Imitation" is as much a morphed reflection of the original as it is an invitation to comparison. So seemingly blasphemous is this poem in its emphasis on the interlacing of spiritual and physical vision that the reader might wish, subsequently, to read again, or for the first time, the 16th-century poet's works.

In this context, Sarduy wrote: mindful not only of his living contemporaries, many of whom he honors in his sonnets, but of those poets who served as models for his writing centuries ago. Considering his final works, Suzanne Jill Levine writes that after the Argentine writer Manuel Puig had died of the virus plaguing primarily gay men at the time, "AIDS victim Reinaldo Arenas, in an advanced stage of illness, committed suicide. With all his friends gone, Severo Sarduy, terrified, knew his turn was next; his last writings bravely and meticulously confronted his own personal struggle with the virus."[13]

In writing this note, I consider now how Sarduy might have imagined the writing of his last stories and poems, abbreviated by illness and left, possibly, to be translated after his death. Sarduy's final novel, *Pájaros en la playa* (*Beach Birds*) was published soon after his passing in 1993, and its translation was published in 2007. The text offers insight into the disease and the author's relationship to the island, perhaps of his birth, though both the disease and the island remain unnamed. Despite the novel's deliberate occlusion of those two proper nouns, the work's translators, Suzanne Jill Levine and Carol Maier, write that the "colonial island" where the plot takes place is "filled with disease-infested birds, [and] a large crumbling mansion serves as a refuge and hospital for young men prematurely withered by illness."[14] The same translators flag "a 'late style' reminiscent of the 'untimely... last or late period of life' described by Edward Said," and they contend, therein, that "Sarduy achieved a style unlike the one that preceded it, one whose rigor would both resemble and differ from his earlier work."[15]

Likewise, Sarduy's final *décimas*—10-line stanzas or poems following a strict, Baroque rhyme scheme with roots in the 16th century—were published after the author's passing and, in their title—"Epitafios" ("Epitaphs")[16]—cut to the chase in their allusions to death, even in jocularity and even as death's arrival appears to remain incomplete. The fifth epitaph in this series speaks apostrophically to the figure meant to stand in for the absence of life:

Death, you are so lazy
in delivering your sentence
—here rests your witness—.

In these lines, syllabically briefer than those of a sonnet, an immediate concern for death is juxtaposed, notably, with a concern for death's deferred delivery. Perhaps more hopefully, the first epitaph in the same section renders a comparable gesture to the afterlife in the following words, when the poem's narrator, again, speaks from, or of, his grave:

Here lies, deaf and severe,
he who used so many shoes'
soles, whose hips he abused

from the front and from behind.
Laconic adagio—and soothsayer—
inscribe on his tomb
—the skeleton crumbles,
gold of jewels undone—:
his name, and between two dates,
"the dead man's out to dance."

Typical of the poet's dramatization of puns, the first line in Spanish writes the author's name into the text with the word "severe," which, in Spanish, is "severo." The poems' spirited ruminations on the grave are not merely songs to the dead, but enlivening celebrations of the body, of a man whose moving feet wore out his shoes, of poetry and how it, too, can be given life in one's attempt to interpret, re-write, or imitate the works of those no longer living. The epitaph concludes, too, with exultation in dance. Rather than writing further on Sarduy's poems in prosaic terms, I leave the reader to explore them—their imitations—in translation.

Notes

1. For more regarding the question of (Cuban) identity—in relationship to traditional Latin American novels and Sarduy's innovative forms— read Roberto González Echevarría's introduction to *De dónde son los cantantes*, 4th ed. (Madrid: Ediciones Cátedra, 2005). Note, in particular, González Echevarría's argument that, "Sarduy's novels are—as ludicrous as it may seem—very historical, either because they represent with relative fidelity an international underworld of popular culture, drugs, and sex, or because they reflect or perhaps interpret vast historical movements. For example, the deformations of characters represent those that are a result of the West's morbid desire for the East..., an East that is a projection of that desire, and that remains condemned always to a twisted and superficial version of its cultures." "Las novelas de Sarduy son—por muy disparatado que parezca—muy históricas, tanto porque representan con relativa fidelidad un submundo internacional de cultura popular, drogas, y sexo, como porque reflejan o tal vez interpretan vastos movimientos históricos. Por ejemplo, las deformaciones de los personajes representan aquellas que resultan del mórbido deseo del Occidente por el Oriente..., un Oriente que es una proyección de ese deseo, y que queda condenado a una versión siempre tergiversada y superficial de sus culturas" (25). Translation mine.
2. Richard Howard, review on book jacket. Severo Sarduy, *Cobra* and *Maitreya*, trans. Suzanne Jill Levine (Normal, IL: Dalkey Archive Press, 1995).
3. Justo Barranco, "Las obras completas de Severo Sarduy muestran la relevancia de sus poesías y sus ensayos," *La Vanguardia Digital*, December 9, 2009, *https://www.cubanet.org/htdocs/CNews/y99/dec99/0909.htm*.
4. For more on this concept, see Severo Sarduy, *Written on a Body*, trans. Carol Maier (New York: Lumen Books, 1989).
5. J. Edgar Bauer, "*Cabio Sile Changó!*: On Severo Sarduy's Archaeology of Negritude and the Post-modern Reassessment of the Orisha Cult," in *In and Out of Africa: Exploring Afro-Hispanic, Luso-Brazilian, and Latin-American Connections*, ed. Joanna Boampong (Newcastle upon Tyne: Cambridge Scholars Publishing), 154.
6. Roberto González Echevarría, *La ruta de Severo Sarduy*, 2nd ed. (Leiden: Almenara Press, 2017), 27.

7. "Lubricate," Online Etymology Dictionary, *https://www.etymonline.com/word/lubricate?ref=etymonline_crossreference#etymonline_v_14574*.
8. Cited in Peter G. Earle's "The Essay," in *A History of Literature in the Caribbean: Volume 1: Hispanic and Francophone Regions*, ed. A. James Arnold, Julio Rodriguez-Luis, and J. Michael Dash (Amsterdam: John Benjamins Publishing Company), 274.
9. "Aporia," Online Etymology Dictionary, *https://www.etymonline.com/search?q=aporia*.
10. "*Aporía*," *Diccionario de la lengua española*, Real Academia Española, Edición del Tricentenario, 2019, *https://dle.rae.es/apor%C3%ADa*. The definition, in Spanish, is, "Enunciado que expresa o que contiene una inviabilidad de orden racional."
11. "Cipher," Online Etymology Dictionary, *https://www.etymonline.com/search?q=cipher*.
12. The original, in Spanish, reads, "La otra actitud posible, por definición blasfematoria o infatuada, es la de librarse a una imitación. Mímesis en lugar de lectura; doble y simulacro en lugar de interpretación. Reflejo, forzosamente deformado, del divino epitalamio. Ir en la copia hacia la materialización de las metáforas, explicitar las elipsis, recorrer otra vez el camino: desde el cuerpo enardecido hasta Dios, desde el deseo hasta la fusión con el Uno...." Severo Sarduy, *Obras I: Poesía* (Mexico City: Fondo de Cultura Económica, 2007), 185.
13. Suzanne Jill Levine, *Manuel Puig and the Spider Woman: His Life and Fictions* (New York: Farrar, Straus and Giroux, 2000), 376.
14. Suzanne Jill Levine and Carol Maier, "Translators' Afterward," *Beach Birds* by Severo Sarduy (Los Angeles: Otis Books, 2007), 174.
15. Ibid, 181.
16. Included in *Últimos poemas* in Severo Sarduy, *Obras I: Poesía* (Mexico City: Fondo de Cultura Económica, 2007).

Acknowledgements

Grateful acknowledgement to the editors of *Inventory* and *Exchanges: Journal of Literary Translation* for publishing earlier versions of some of these works.

I wish to express my gratitude to my family and also to friends, writers, and scholars, Anne Stachura, Juan Acevedo, Jennifer Chang, John D'Amico, Kim Icreverzi, Jenny Johnson, Ricardo Maldonado, Billy Merrell, Stephanie Pridgeon, Yvette Siegert, Lisa Russ Spaar, Matthew Tanico, and Justin Quarry, all of whom supported this work along the way. I have immense gratitude for my scholarly mentors at Harvard, Brad Epps, Alice Jardine, Mark Jordan, Sergio Delgado, Mariano Siskind, Doris Sommer, Mary Gaylord, Nicolau Sevcenko, and Christy McDonald, whose questions on the thinking of writing, sexuality, and multilingualism—often through Sarduy—gave me a deeper understanding of the intellectual underpinnings of Sarduy's work. My thanks to Gustavo Pellón for encouraging my first readings of *Daiquirí*. Roberto González Echevarría's feedback on final versions of these poems brought new clarity to Sarduy's corpus as a whole. Thanks, also, to the librarians at Princeton and the Friends of Princeton University Library, whose research grant allowed me to study their collection of the poet's remarkable paintings. I am indebted to Grace Hopper College and Julia Adams for making Yale a true academic community. And I am grateful to Alicia Schmidt Camacho and Yale's Program in Ethnicity, Race, and Migration, particularly to its students, for providing a place in the classroom to discuss the migratory movements of narrative through poetry and translation. Special thanks to Jennifer Kronovet and Dan Visel—for their editorial brilliance and for giving these poems a home.

BIG BANG

(1974)

BIG BANG

(1974)

FLAMENCO

FLAMENCO

Polígonos de estuco. Cúpulas que en el agua reflejan. A cada cuerda tiembla la superficie, a cada voz en el rectángulo de la alberca se desplaza un instante la sucesión de arcos, de salas que se abren al jardín, de jardines idénticos que interrumpen albercas, rectángulos espejeantes, agua inmóvil donde a cada voz, a cada cuerda se reflejan un instante, desaparecen, se reflejan otra vez los vacíos polígonos de estuco, las cúpulas, madera y nácar, la invariable sucesión de los arcos, el orden de las salas sonoras, los jardines florecidos, húmedos, abandonados saqueados, devastados, quemados, olvidados, ruinas, sueños, cenizas.

Stucco polygons. Cupulas reflected on the water. At each chord the surface trembles, at the sound of each voice in the rectangular swimming pool a succession of arches expands from rooms that open to the garden, from identical gardens that interrupt swimming pools, rectangular glimmers, still water wherein each voice, each chord is reflected for a moment, disappears, the water reflecting again the empty stucco polygons, the cupulas, wood and mother of pearl, the invariable succession of arches, the order of resounding rooms, the flowering gardens, humid, abandoned, plundered, razed, burnt, forgotten ruins, dreams, ashes.

Las páginas cuberitas de letras de oro. Al paso del lector la luz cernida por dátiles refleja los signos sobre el muro, un instante sobre la arena negra. A cada movimiento de la mano, a cada nueva página la escritura aparece sobre las cenefas, entre las piedras rojas y otra vez sobre el muro,
							a lo largo
del muro donde el mapa de la página anterior acaba de borrarse, los signos descendiendo hacia la arena, brasas.

The pages covered in gold letters. When the reader passes, light sifting through his fingers reflects signs on the wall, an instant over the black sand. At each movement of the hand, at each new page, the writing appears on the borders, between the red stones and again on the wall,

                                        along the wall

where the previous page's map was just erased, the signs descending on the sand, embers.

El agua une sus vidrios, cubre los rombos negros. Sobre el azulejo van apareciendo las sombras, los gestos, el rondel de las cúpulas.

                                          Ya repercuten
los oros, los rostros visibles a cada golpe de agua.
En los jardines negros
            entre columnas húmedas,
            los conos de las tumbas.

Water weds to windows, covers black diamonds. Over the tiles, shadows, the gestures, the cupulas' rondel begin to appear.
                                                The gold colors and visible faces rebound at each slap of water.
In the black gardens
        among humid columns,
           the cones on their tombs.

El coro chillón, el golpe de los bronces oxidados; arena empaña los vidrios.

Una mano se alza y entonces se oyen los sopranos, agua verde rodando sobre latas, sobre metales cada vez más finos, entre cubos de cornetas mohosas,

                      hasta que el hilo estridente se pierde entre las manchas de musgo, siguiendo una línea de puntos.

The piercing chorus, the blow of oxidized bronzes; sand coats the windows.

A hand rises and you can hear the sopranos, green water rolling over tin plates, over metals ever finer, through buckets of moldy cornets,
                        until the shrill trickle is lost in the moss stains, following a dotted line.

muros blancos
muros blancos
muros blancos
muros blancos
muros blancos
           puertas negras
lejana y/o sola

white walls
white walls
white walls
white walls
white walls
          black doors
distant and/or alone

	COMO UNA PIEDRA NEGRA
sobre la cal la sombra	
	SOBRE UNA PIEDRA BLANCA
añil de los jardines	
	COMO FIBRA DE VIDRIO
en los sonoros patios	
	TAPANDO UNA VENTANA
las letras se repiten	
	HERRERÍA BARROCA
formando una cenefa	
	SOBRE LA CAL LA SOMBRA
(las palabras son muros)	
	COLORES DILATADOS
la espiral de la frase	
	HIERROS ENTRELAZÁNDOSE
al fijarse, una cúpula	
	ARABESCOS HERÁLDICOS
la página, una sala	
	DOBLE QUE EL SOL DESPLAZA
(el palacio es un libro)	
	SOBRE CAMPO DE CAL
a la vez piedra y letra	
	ESCRIBIENDO LAS ARMAS
pensamiento y soporte	
	ENTRE CUERDAS LAS LETRAS
armazón y sentido	
	SOBRE LOS MUROS BLANCOS
la escritura va armando	
	SI LOS DIBUJOS CAMBIAN
edificios de signos	
	REVERSO DE LA LUZ
las letras se repiten	
	PARA MEDIR EL DÍA
el palacio es un libro	
la exactitud del agua	

      LIKE A BLACK STONE
   over the shadow's lime
      OVER A WHITE STONE
  the gardens' indigo
      LIKE A FIBERGLASS
 in the echoing patios
      COVERING A WINDOW
 the letters repeat
      BAROQUE IRONWORK
 forming a border
      THE SHADOW OVER LIME
 (the words are walls)
      DILATED COLORS
 spiral of the phrase
      INTERLACING IRONS
 when fixed, a cupula
      HERALDIC ARABESQUES
the page, a room
      DOUBLE THE SUN DISPLACES
(the palace is a book)
      OVER A FIELD OF LIME
 at once, stone and letter
      WRITING WEAPONS
 thought and foundation
      BETWEEN CORDS LETTERS
  framework and meaning
      OVER THE WHITE WALLS
  the writing builds itself
      IF THE DRAWINGS CHANGE
  buildings made of signs
      THE OTHER SIDE OF LIGHT
  the letters repeat themselves
      TO MEASURE THE DAY
   the palace is a book
    the precision of water

Este río
                        ENTRE LOS MOLINOS ÁRABES
                                    hoy endebles maderas
convirtiéndose en otro
                        SE BAÑABAN LOS PRÍNCIPES
                                    las aspas despegadas
como el agua en agua
                        ALJÓFAR LA FILTRABA
                                    los muchachos de Córdoba
las cambiantes arenas
                        EL ORO DE LAS TÚNICAS
                                    en carretas los órganos
fue bautizado Duero
                        SOBRE NOBLES ARENAS
                                    vendedores de dulces
el duero en el genil
                        YA QUE NO SON DORADAS
                                    en el patio los niños
el genil en el tajo
                        EL INCA GARCILASO
                                    jugando a que jugaban
el tajo en el guadiana
                        TAMBORILES Y DÁTILES
                                    entre los capiteles
el guadiane en el sena
                        SU NOMBRE EN UN SONETO
                                    se esconden los fotógrafos
el sena en orinoco
                        TALLADORES DE PIEDRA
                                    columnas de vinil
el orinoco en nilo
                        LOS SUCESIVOS ARCOS
                                    operetas morescas
el nilo en amazonas
                        QUE GÓNGORA ESCRIBIERA
                                    con guitarras eléctricas
el amazonas ganges
                        LLAMABAN LOS ALMUÉDANOS
                                    caravanas trilingües
el ganges en el mar
                        POLÍGONO ESTRELLADO
                                    filmada en tecnicolor
la corriente es inmóvil
                        LEJANA Y SOLA CÓRDOBA
                                    minrab de bakelita
la rivera la misma
                        LAS VENTANAS ROSADAS
                                    ruinas de poliéster
todo acto es ilusorio
                        COLUMNAS DE PORFIRIO
                                    la cúpula es inflable
circular como tiempo
                        DICE: "SÓLO DIOS VENCE"
                                    estrellas de neón.

Fandangos

Fandangos

    This river
                    BETWEEN ARABIC MILLS
                                 today of rickety wood
    turning itself into another
                    THE PRINCES WERE BATHING
                                 blades detached
    like water into water
                    THE PEARL FILTERED IT
                                 young men of Córdoba
    the shifting sands
                    THE GOLD OF TUNICS
                                 organs in wagons
    was baptized Douro
                    ON NOBLE SANDS
                                 vendors of candies
    the douro in the genil
                    NOW THAT THEY ARE NO LONGER GOLD
                               the children on the patio
    the genil in the tagus
                    THE INCA GARCILASO
                               playing what they played
    the tagus in the guadiana
                    TABORS AND HANDS
                               among the columns' capitals
    the guadiana in the seine
                    HIS NAME IN A SONNET
                               the photographers are hidden
    the seine in the orinoco
                    CARVERS OF STONE
                               columns of vinyl
    the orinoco in the nile
                    THE CONTINUOUS ARCHES
                               Moorish operettas
    the nile in the amazon
                    THAT GÓNGORA WOULD WRITE
                               with electric guitars
    the amazon ganges
                    THE MUEZZINS WERE CALLING
                               trilingual caravans
    the ganges in the sea
                    STAR-SHAPED POLYGON
                               filmed in technicolor
    the current is still
                    CÓRDOBA DISTANT AND ALONE
                               mihrab of bakelite
    the brook the same
                    THE WINDOWS PINK
                               polyester ruins
    every act is illusory
                    COLUMNS OF PORPHYRY
                               the cupola is inflatable
    circular as time
                    SAYS: "GOD ALONE CONQUERS"
                               neon stars.

BIG BANG FLAMENCO

                        entre molinos árabes
                        HOY ENDEBLES MADERAS
                        este río
                        LAS ASPAS DESPEGADAS
                    convirtiéndose en otro
                        LOS MUCHACHOS DE CÓRDOBA
                como el agua en el agua
                        EN CARRETA LOS ÓRGANOS
            las cambiantes arenas
                        VENDEDORES DE DULCE
            fue bautizado Duero
                        EN EL PATIO LOS NIÑOS
            el duero en el genil
                        JUGANDO A QUE JUGABAN
            el genil en el tajo
                        ENTRE LOS CAPITELES
            el tajo en el guadiana
                        SE ESCONDEN LOS FOTÓGRAFOS
        el Guadiana en el sena
                        COLUMNAS DE VINIL
    se bañaban los príncipes
                        ALJÓFAR LAS FILTRABA

            ORO DE LAS TÚNICAS SOBRE NOBLES ARENAS
                                    operetas morescas
                EL SENA EN ORINOCO
                                con guitarras eléctricas
                EL ORINOCO EN NILO
                                caravanas trilingües
                EL NILO EN AMAZONAS
                                filmada en tecnicolor
                EL AMAZONAS GANGES
                                minrab de bakelita
                EL GANGES EN EL MAR
                            ruinas de poliéster
                LA CORRIENTE ES INMÓVIL
                            la cúpula es inflable
                LA RIVERA LA MISMA
                        estrellas de neón
                TODO ACTO ILUSORIO
                    Córdoba's drug store
                CIRCULAR COMO EL TIEMPO
                    Poster del Cordobés
                DICE: "SÓLO DIOS VENCE"

                between Arabic mills
            TODAY OF RICKETY WOOD
                    this river
            THE BLADES DETACHED
        turning itself into another
            THE YOUNG MEN OF CÓRDOBA
        like water into water
                        ORGANS IN WAGONS
            the shifting sands
                            CANDY VENDORS
        was baptized Douro
                THE CHILDREN ON THE PATIO
        the douro in the genil
                    PLAYING WHAT THEY PLAYED
        the genil in the tagus
                    AMONG THE COLUMN'S CAPITALS
        the tagus in the guadiana
                    THE PHOTOGRAPHERS ARE HIDDEN
        the guadiana in the seine
                                COLUMNS OF VINYL
        the princes were bathing   THE PEARL FILTERED THEM

        GOLD OF TUNICS ON THE NOBLE SANDS
                                Moorish operettas
            THE SEINE IN THE ORINOCO
                                with electric guitars
            THE ORINOCO IN THE NILE
                                trilingual caravans
            THE NILE IN THE AMAZON
                                filmed in technicolor
            THE AMAZON GANGES
                            mihrab of bakelite
            THE GANGES IN THE SEA
                        polyester ruins
            THE CURRENT IS STILL
                        the cupola is inflatable
            THE BROOK THE SAME
                        neon stars
            EVERY ILLUSORY ACT
                    Córdoba's drug store
            CIRCULAR AS TIME
                The Córdovan's poster
            SAYS: "GOD ALONE CONQUERS"

Tientos

por donde hacia la luz huye el sonido
                                          ALJÓFAR BLANCO
en sucesivas cámaras de eco
                                          NO SÓLO EN PLATA
convertidos los cuerpos y guitarra
                                          EN TIERRA, EN HUMO

las cuerdas prolongadas
                                          O CUAL POR MANOS HECHA, ARTIFICIOSAS
mecánicas sonoras
                                          DESTINADA SEÑAL QUE MORDIÓ AGUDA
volúmenes de ocre
                                          BREVE URNA LOS SELLA COMO HUESOS

Tientos

where light falls, sound runs
                        WHITE PEARL
in consecutive echo chambers
                        NOT ONLY IN SILVER
bodies and guitar converted
                        IN EARTH, IN SMOKE

the chords prolonged
                        OR MADE ARTIFICIAL BY HANDS
sonorous mechanics
                        DESTINED GESTURE WHICH BIT WITH A HIGH PITCH
volumes of ochre
                        BRIEF URN SEALS THEM AS BONES

Sevillanas

   EN EL ESPACIO DE LO BLANCO, donde las sombras se anulan, la luz va royendo los bordes, plegando los colores, destruyendo las formas,
   EN EL ESPACIO DE LO BLANCO, pasando del otro lado de la banda, irrumpiendo en el ámbito sin límites (sin sombras)
    esfera
    rectángulo amarillo, manchas verdes
    triángulo, convergencia del iris
    piezas cuyo mármol es apenas visible
         se dibujan,
son ganados otra vez por la luz, descompuestos, expulsados de la página, figura desunida, apagada, que
   EN EL ESPACIO DE LO BLANCO, un instante después va insinuando sus formas, creando las franjas de color, definiendo sus bordes, apareciendo ya a medida en que la excesiva luz se retira:
    una cabeza,
    un cuadrado azafrán, óvalos azules y verdes,
    un prisma,
    un cuerpo segmentado.

Blanco

Sevillanas

   IN THE WHITE SPACE, where shadows are annulled, light goes gnawing at the borders, folding the colors, destroying the forms,
   IN THE WHITE SPACE, crossing over from the other side of the band of light, bursting in without limits (without shadows)
> sphere
> yellow rectangle, green stains
> triangle, convergence of the iris
> pieces whose marble is hardly visible
>> are drawn,

are won over once more by the light, decomposed, expelled from the page, disjointed figure, extinguished, that
   IN THE WHITE SPACE, an instant later goes insinuating its forms, creating fringes of color, defining their borders, appearing while the excessive light withdraws:
> a head,
> a squared saffron, blue and green ovals,
> a prism,
> a segmented body.

White

Tanguillo

un prisma la cabeza
                    QUE PRIVILEGIA EL CIELO Y DORA EL DÍA
las rayas del tablado
                    DE ARENAS NOBLES YA QUE NO DORADAS
ceñido fieltro verde
                    TU MEMORIA NO FUE ALIMENTO MÍO

        un prisma transparente estría el rojo
                          OH TORRES CORONADAS
        que las rayas apresan, sombra breve
                          OH FÉRTIL LLANO
        y en ese fieltro se dibuja el paso
                          OH FLOR DE ESPAÑA!

Tanguillo

the head a prism
    THAT PRIVILEGES THE SKY AND GILDS THE DAY
the planks on the stage
    OF NOBLE SANDS NOW THAT THEY'RE NO LONGER GILDED
tight-fitting green felt
    YOUR MEMORY WAS NOT MY NOURISHMENT

    a transparent prism striates the red
        OH CROWNED TOWERS
    that the planks capture, brief shadow
        OH FERTILE PLAIN
    and in that felt the step is drawn
        OH SPANISH FLOWER!

Seguidillas

si las haces girar
                naranja   LIMÓN   cereza
unas sobre otras
                LIMÓN   cereza   LIMÓN
las piezas invisibles
                cereza   LIMÓN   LIMÓN
si coinciden
                cereza   LIMÓN   LIMÓN
los segmentos
                LIMÓN   naranja   LIMÓN
que un adamiaje fija
                naranja   LIMÓN   LIMÓN
si al detenerse
                LIMÓN   cereza   LIMÓN
unas sobre otras
                naranja   LIMÓN   LIMÓN
las invisibles piezas
                naranja   LIMÓN   LIMÓN
se continúan sus líneas
                                  despúes de un golpe seco
                LIMÓN   LIMÓN   LIMÓN
                                  cascada de monedas

        Habrás armado un cuerpo

Seguidillas

if you make them spin
                       orange   LEMON   cherry
some over others
                       LEMON   cherry   LEMON
the invisible pieces
                       cherry   LEMON   LEMON
if they coincide
                       cherry   LEMON   LEMON
the segments
                       LEMON   orange   LEMON
that a framework fixes
                       orange   LEMON   LEMON
if once they stop
                       LEMON   cherry   LEMON
some over the others
                       orange   LEMON   LEMON
the invisible pieces
                       orange   LEMON   LEMON
their lines carry on
                                                            after a dry thud
                       LEMON   LEMON   LEMON
                                                              cascade of coins

        You will have built a body

Alegrías

un triángulo de estratos
        SE LE FUE EL AZOGUE
                tablado verde
mármoles divergentes
        COMO ESCRIBIR EN AGUA
                el cuerpo gira
un prisma la cabeza
        QUE ESTÁ EN LO ALTO DE LA TORRE
                sobre lentes mojados
el cuerpo es una máquina
        CON LOS DÍAS DE INVIERNO
                la pierna una hélice
en equilibrio estable
        UN LETRERO QUE DICE
                relojería blanca

Alegrías

a triangle of strata
    THE MERCURY LEFT IT
        green floorboard
divergent marble
    LIKE WRITING IN WATER
        the body spins
the head a prism
    THAT IS AT THE TOP OF THE TOWER
        over wet glasses
the body is a machine
    WITH THE DAYS OF WINTER
        the leg a propeller
in stable equilibrium
    A SIGN THAT SAYS
        watchmaker's white shop

Zapateado

A la luz amarilla aparecen un instante, se borran, superpuestos a sí mismos, divididos por una falla negra, los volúmenes de ocre, los cuerpos vacíos que lo negro, la sombra espesa sobre la página tacha, deja ver un instante más hasta que la luz amarilla, limón, ópalo, vidrio de orine, acecho de ojos de tigre vuelve a descubrirnos, a extraerlos del fondo de la página, de la noche de tinta, a rescatarlos para le efímera simetría que ordena una línea, que divide una falla negra a cuyos lados se equilibran cuerpos de ocre, volúmenes vacíos que esplenderán un instante, estampados de amarillo, día estriado, salto, azufre, tigre.

Zapateado

Beneath the yellow light, they appear for another instant, then disappear, superimposed over each other, divided by a black break, volumes of ochre, empty bodies that the blackness, the thick shadow on the blemished page, reveals for an instant until the yellow, lemon, opal, piss glass, spying tiger-eyes light returns to discover us, extracting them from the depths of the page, from the night of ink, to rescue them for the ephemeral symmetry that orders a line, that divides a black break at whose sides ochre bodies equalize, empty volumes that will become resplendent for another instant, printed in yellow, striated day, leap, sulfur, tiger.

Farruca

DENTRO DE UN CUBO BLANCO
aristas superpuestas
anamorfosis del espacio
                    EL CUERPO
                    volúmenes de ocre
                    superficies grisáceas
                              ENARBOLA SUS CAJAS

        el cuerpo es un volumen
        dimensiones opacas

        el cuerpo es un sistema
        que un andamiaje fija

        el cuerpo es una máquina
        dentro de un cubo blanco

Farruca

INSIDE A WHITE CUBE
superimposed edges
anamorphosis of space
                      THE BODY
                      volumes of ochre
                      grayish surfaces
                              LIFTS ITS BOXES

      the body is a volume
      opaque dimensions

      the body is a system
      that a framework fixes

      the body is a machine
      inside a white cube

            DENTRO DE UN CUBO BLANCO   el cuerpo es un volumen
              ARISTAS SUPERPUESTAS
            EL CUERPO   dimensiones opacas
          ANAMORFOSIS DEL ESPACIO
          ENARBOLA SUS CAJAS   el cuerpo es un sistema
        EL CUERPO ES UNA MÁQUINA
        EL CUERPO ES UN VOLUMEN   que un andamiaje fija
             VOLÚMENES DE OCRE
        DIMENSIONES OPACAS   el cuerpo es una máquina
            SUPERFICIES GRISÁCEAS
        EL CUERPO ES UN SISTEMA   dentro de un cubo blanco
        DENTRO DE UN CUBO BLANCO
        QUE UN ANDAMIAJE FIJA   aristas superpuestas
                      EL CUERPO
        EL CUERPO ES UNA MÁQUINA   anamorfosis del espacio
            ENARBOLA SUS CAJAS
        DENTRO DE UN CUBO BLANCO   volúmenes de ocre
          UN VOLUMEN FICTICIO
        LA PÁGINA ES UN CUBO   superficies grisáceas
            CÓMPLICE LA MIRADA
        TODO CUERPO ES UN CUBO   dentro de un cubo blanco
            VOLÚMENES DE OCRE
        TODO CUBO UNA ESFERA   el cuerpo
            SUPERFICIES GRISÁCEAS
        TODO CUERPO CONVIERTE   dentro de un cubo blanco
        DENTRO DE UN CUBO BLANCO
        SUS ARISTAS EN OTROS   el cuerpo
                    el cuerpo
                    enarbola sus cajas

INSIDE A WHITE CUBE	the body is a volume
SUPERIMPOSED EDGES	
THE BODY	opaque dimensions
ANAMORPHOSIS OF SPACE	
LIFTS ITS BOXES	the body is a system
THE BODY IS A MACHINE	
THE BODY IS A VOLUME	that a framework fixes
VOLUMES OF OCHRE	
OPAQUE DIMENSIONS	the body is a machine
GRAYISH SURFACES	
THE BODY IS A SYSTEM	inside a white cube
INSIDE A WHITE CUBE	
THAT A FRAMEWORK FIXES	superimposed edges
THE BODY	
THE BODY IS A MACHINE	anamorphosis of space
LIFTS ITS BOXES	
INSIDE A WHITE CUBE	volumes of ochre
A FICTIVE VOLUME	
THE PAGE IS A CUBE	grayish surfaces
THE GAZE AN ACCOMPLICE	
EVERY BODY IS A CUBE	inside a white cube
VOLUMES OF OCHRE	
EVERY CUBE IS A SPHERE	the body
GRAYISH SURFACES	
EVERY BODY CHANGES	inside a white cube
INSIDE A WHITE CUBE	
ITS EDGES IN OTHERS	the body

        the body
            lifts its boxes

Mineras

    el fieltro carmelita
                      frente al muro de oro
                                      volúmenes de ocre
    el verdín
                la sombra redondeada
                          que un andamiaje fija
    han tapizado el muro
                soldada a un cubo negro
                PIEDRA YA NO GUITARRA

Mineras

the Carmelite felt
                in front of the golden wall
                              volumes of ochre
the mossy green
                the rounded shadow
                              that a framework fixes
they've covered the wall
                welded to a black cube
                STONE NO LONGER GUITAR

       EL FIELTRO CARMELITA
    polígono estrellado
       EL VERDÍN
     los sucesivos arcos
     HAN TAPIZADO EL MURO
      columnas de porfirio
   LA SOMBRA REDONDEADA
        que Góngora escribiera
   SOLDADA A UN CUBO NEGRO
          lejana y sola Córdoba
  FRENTE AL MURO DE ORO
          el fieltro carmelita
  PIEDRA YA NO GUITARRA
           el verdín
 VOLÚMENES DE OCRE
        han tapizado el muro
QUE UN ANDAMIAJE FIJA
        la sombra redondeada
 POLÍGONO ESTRELLADO
      soldada a un cubo negro
  LOS SUCESSIVOS ARCOS
      frente al muro de oro
  COLUMNAS DE PORFIRIO
     piedra ya no guitarra
  QUE GÓNGORA ESCRIBIERA
     volúmenes de ocre
   LEJANA Y SOLA CÓRDOBA
 que un andamiaje fija
      LLAMABAN LOS ALMUÉDANOS

                    THE CARMELITE FELT
              star-shaped polygon
                    THE MOSSY GREEN
               the continuous arches
              HAVE COVERED THE WALL
                 columns of porphyry
               THE ROUNDED SHADOW
                      that Góngora would write
            WELDED TO A BLACK CUBE
                        Córdoba distant and alone
       IN FRONT OF THE GOLDEN WALL
                              the Carmelite felt
      STONE NO LONGER GUITAR
                              the mossy green
     VOLUMES OF OCHRE
                      they've covered the wall
 THAT A FRAMEWORK FIXES
                    the rounded shadow
       STAR-SHAPED POLYGON
                 welded to a black cube
        THE CONTINUOUS ARCHES
                in front of the golden wall
           COLUMNS OF PORPHYRY
                stone no longer guitar
             THAT GÓNGORA WOULD WRITE
              volumes of ochre
              CÓRDOBA DISTANT AND ALONE
      that a framework fixes
                    THE MUEZZINS WERE CALLING

BIG BANG FLAMENCO

Bulerías

      EN EL CUADRADO ROJO
(en un bloque los dedos)
      EL CUERPO ESTÁ ENCERRADO
(en la página el paso)

            FRAGMENTOS DE ALUMINIO
            (urna sino escultura)

CAJAS DE AZOGUE

    en el cuadrado rojo
        (LAS UÑAS OVALADAS)

fragmentos de aluminio
(RECIPIENTES OPACOS)
        el cuerpo está encerrado
        (MOLDE CONVEXO CÓNCAVO)

    cajas de azogue

Bulerías

    IN THE RED SQUARE
(the fingers in a block)
THE BODY IS LOCKED IN
(the step on the page)

                FRAGMENTS OF ALUMINUM
                (urn if not sculpture)

BOXES OF MERCURY

    in the red square
        (THE FINGERNAILS ROUNDED)

fragments of aluminium
(OPAQUE RECIPIENTS)
        the body is locked in
        (CONVEX CONCAVE MOLD)

    boxes of mercury

MOOD INDIGO

MOOD INDIGO

Magenta Haze

RUMOR DE BOBINAS GIRANDO

RUMOR DE BOBINAS GIRANDO

RUMOR DE BOBINAS GIRANDO
                                                                luz mostazarectángulo
RUMOR DE BOBINAS GIRANDO
                                     puntos negros temblando
RUMOR DE BOBINAS GIRANDO
                           dibujan   desdibujan
RUMOR DE BOBINAS GIRANDO
                  sobre lo blanco blanco
RUMOR DE BOBINAS GIRANDO

RUMOR DE BOBINAS GIRANDO

RUMOR DE celuloide quemad o

RUMOR DE BOBINAS GIRANDO

RUMOR DE BOBINAS GIRANDO
                  flash boca recta número
RUMOR DE BOBINAS GIRANDO
                            luz letrero borrad o
RUMOR DE BOBINAS GIRANDO
                                 crines cifra porosa
RUMOR DE BOBINAS GIRANDO
                                       los bordes perforados
RUMOR DE BOBINAS GIRANDO

RUMOR DE BOBINAS GIRANDO

RUMOR DE BOBINAS GIRANDO

Magenta Haze

MURMUR OF SPINNING SPOOLS

MURMUR OF SPINNING SPOOLS

MURMUR OF SPINNING SPOOLS
                                                     light mustardrectangle
MURMUR OF SPINNING SPOOLS
                                   black points trembling
MURMUR OF SPINNING SPOOLS
                              drawing   blurring
MURMUR OF SPINNING SPOOLS
                 above the white white
MURMUR OF SPINNING SPOOLS

MURMUR OF SPINNING SPOOLS

MURMUR OF burnt celluloi d

MURMUR OF SPINNING SPOOLS

MURMUR OF SPINNING SPOOLS
            flash straight mouth number
MURMUR OF SPINNING SPOOLS
                        light sign erase d
MURMUR OF SPINNING SPOOLS
                              manes porous code
MURMUR OF SPINNING SPOOLS
                                    the borders perforated
MURMUR OF SPINNING SPOOLS

MURMUR OF SPINNING SPOOLS

MURMUR OF SPINNING SPOOLS

The Mooche

incrustarte cascabeles en las mejillas
con cal escribirte en la frente
con rayas espirales pintarte el sexo
las nalgas con discos fluorescentes

                                      líneas de puntos blancos
                                      agrimensor de tu cuerpo negro

firmarte la cabeza
cubrirte los pies de yeso
flores de oro en las manos
ojos egipcios en el pecho

                                      ideogramas blancos
                                      un mapa negro de tu cuerpo

The Mooche

to embed bells in your cheeks
to write with chalk on your forehead
to paint your sex with spiralled lines
your breasts with fluorescent discs

                                        lines of white dots
                                        surveyor of your black body

sign your head
cover your feet with gypsum
golden flowers in the hands
Egyptian eyes on the chest

                                        white ideograms
                                        a black map of your body

Blue Reverie

Cootie Williams a la trompeta-fémur.
Joe Nanton al trombón: para obtener un buen wa-wa
                orine en la boca de cobre.
Johnny Hodges al saxo alto: un gran lama, sí señor. Quién sino
                podría expulsar por la boca
                el aire aspirado por el ano?
Harry Carney al saxo barítono: un gran lama, sí señor. Quién sino
                podría expulsar por el ano
                el aire aspirado por la boca?
Sonny Greer al drum: los tamborines:
                    cráneos de niño serruchados por la mitad
                    cuero de yack legítimo.
Duke al piano en llamas.

TANTRIC ORCHESTRA

Blue Reverie

Cootie Williams on the thighbone trumpet.
Joe Nanton on the trombone: to get a good wa-wa
                            piss in the copper mouth.
Johnny Hodges on the alto sax: a great lama, yes sir. Who if not him
                       could expel from his mouth
                       air aspirated in the ass?
Harry Carney on the baritone sax: a great lama, yes sir. Who if not him
                        could expel from his ass
                       air aspirated in the mouth?
Sonny Greer on the drum: the tambourines:
                       children's skulls sawed in half
                       authentic yak leather.
Duke at the piano on fire.

Sophisticated Lady

                        con el trombón de Benny Morton
                          y la trompeta de Dizzy Gillespie
                              probado por expertos catadores
               droga   con sudor negro
           danza   en la cala de un barco
                              en un barco de ruedas

otra vez fetiche
   de tan sofisticada
      tan de oro y dobles arabescos
         de piedras y plumas incrustada   dios
            cubo de marfil   puntos negros   dado
               una trompeta oxidada

Sophisticated Lady

                        with Benny Morton's trombone
                          and Dizzy Gillespie's trumpet
                              tested by those with expertise
            drug   with black sweat
       dance   in a ship's cove
                                    in a steamship

another fetish
   of such sophistication
      such gold and doubled arabesques
         incrusted in stones and feathers   god
            ivory cube   black dots   given
               an oxidized trumpet

Moon Mist

                                                                   antilope
                                                                    ornamentos

                                  el aduanero
                                  sueña
                                  serpiente
                                  flauta
              cubierto de cuños rojos
              rayado, veloz
              de un tigre que pasa
              rumor de orquídeas pudriéndose

SOL filtrado por una empalizada   bambú
     barcos de rueda—la orquesta a bordo—:reflejo de cobres   SOL

                    fetiche salpicado semen coágulos
                    piedras blancas los ojos
                    en el templo de Ochúm
                                ámbar
                                junto al río
                                inmóvil
                                caracoles girando

                                                    amuletos
                                                de ópalo

Moon Mist

                                          antelope
                                          ornaments

                       the customs officer
                       dreams
                       snake
                       flute
    covered with red stamps
    striped, fast
    with a tiger passing by
    rumor of rotting orchids

SUN filtered through a bamboo   palisade
    steamships—the orchestra on board—:reflections of copper   SUN

            fetish sprinkled semen clots
            white stones the eyes
            in the temple of Ochum
                          amber
                          beside the river
                          immobile
                          snails turning

                                    amulets
                                  of opal

Echoes of Harlem

                                                          panteras
                                          negras
con postigos cerrados
   con tablones las puertas claveteadas
  con sacos de arena y espejos rotos
    y amuletos cerrando las ventanas

        conjuros matablanco
           Jean Genet en un una maleta olvidada

      ametralladoras
      hay que romperlo todo
    Ecos de Harlem rayado
              ciclón
  pastelitos de hasch
                cero
Nina al piano
            hay que arrasarlo todo

            la próxima vez   fuego!

Echoes of Harlem

                                                        black
                                                    panthers

with shut shutters
   with planks studding doors
      with bags of sand and broken mirrors
         and amulets locking windows

                   incantations murderwhite
                      Jean Genet in a forgotten suitcase

                machine guns
           everything must be broken
          Echoes of striped Harlem
                     cyclone
  little hash cakes
                          zero
Nina at the piano
                                everything must be destroyed

                            the next time   fire!

Golden Feathers

                    con cascabeles roncos
                    con vidrios trizados
            con Cootie Williams a la trompeta
                      y Duke al piano
                en la madera de las claves
            han dejado escrituras yorubas
          las moridas de los perros mudos

tambores dobles	con Ray Nance al violín
clepsidras de ácana y cuero	con Duke al piano
marca al tiempo del jungle	**plumas de oro**
cayendo la ceniza de tus huesos	cayendo la ceniza de tus huesos

Golden Feathers

                with hoarse bells
                with broken glass
                with Cootie Williams on the trumpet
                and Duke at the piano
                on the wood of each key
                they've left Yoruba script
                the bite marks of mute dogs

bongos	with Ray Nance on the violin
leather clepsydra of bullytree wood	with Duke at the piano
marking the jungle's time	**golden feathers**
ash falling from your bones	ash falling from your bones

Tonk

                        negro como la leche
                    como los dientes   negro
                      del mismo negro del agua bautismal
      nieve
                    negro como la página
                        de fibra de cristal   negro
                        córnea de los ojos
  semen

con signos blancos en las mejillas
    cal en la frente
        sin sal para la sed
            en la piel y el hueso
                                ónix
                  espirales blancas tatuadas
                      castillos de plumas en la cabeza
                        un texto en la cara
                          escrito con yeso
                            ébano

Tonk

                black like milk
                    like teeth   black
                        from the same black of baptismal water
    snow
                  black like the page
                      of fiberglass   black
                        cornea of the eyes
semen

with white marks on the cheeks
    chalk on the forehead
        without salt for thirst
            on the skin and bone
                          onyx
                white tattooed spirals
                    castles of flowers on the head
                    a text on the face
                        written with plaster
                      ebony

Mood Indigo *Espiral Negra*

a Piet Mondrian bailando
al woogie-boogie
al boogie-woogie
al Haig
a la Cigale
con elegguas   al Cotton Club
cajas huesos botellas   en los tobillos   al Chori otra vez
bambú de las Antillas   con campanillas   al Tin Angel
frascos llenos de piedras   a Nueva Orleáns   en las muñecas   al Riverside
quijadas de caballo   a La Habana   de la Costa de Oro   al Saint Germain
triángulo banjo cueros   a Congo Square   del Congo a Virginia   al Tabou
con cajas de tabaco   de Nigeria a Río   del centro negro   al Caméléon
al Eddie Condon   de Río a Recife del río   al Half Note
al Central Plaza   los reyes sometidos   con cascabeles   al Chori
al Stuyvesant Casino   las mejillas tatuadas   con castillos de plumas   al Café Bohemia
al Jimmy Ryan's   inmóvil como un río   con pulseras de oro   al Nick's
al Ember's   wasn't dat a wide ribber   spiritual/spiral   al Society
         flechas rojas, minúsculas   al Café Metropole
al Voyager's room   al Birdland
al Composers
al Savoy ballroom   al Carnegie Hall
al Apollo Theater
al Ecole Juillard

Mood Indigo *Black Spiral*

                        to Piet Mondrian dancing
                            to the woogie-boogie
                                to the boogie-woogie
                                  to the Haig
                with Eleguas
                      in the ankles
                          with small bells
                                      to the Cigale
                                         to the Cotton Club
       bamboo from the Antilles
              boxes bones bottles
                                          to the Chori again
         bottles full of stones
                        to Havana
                              to New Orleans
                                     on the wrists
                                                 to the Tin Angel
   horse jawbones
                     to Congo Square
                            from the Golden Coast
                                                 to Riverside
 triangle banjo leathers
                    from Nigeria to Río
                               from the Congo to Virginia
                                               to the Saint Germain
with boxes of tobacco
               from Río to Recife del río
                          from the black center
                                                to the Tabou
to Eddie Condon
             the kings subdued
                          with bells
                                                to the Caméléon
to Central Plaza
            the cheeks tattoed
                        with castles of feathers
                                               to the Half Note
to Stuyvesant Casino
          still as a river
                        bracelets of gold
                                           to the Chori
to Jimmy Ryan's
        wasn't dat a wide ribber
                          red arrows, miniscule
                                          spiritual/spiral
                                                    to Nick's
to Ember's
                                                   to Café Bohemia
    to the Voyager's room
                                 to Birdland
                                             to Café Metropole
       to the Composers
                                             to the Society
          to the Savoy ballroom
              to the Apollo Theater
                       to Carnegie Hall
                to Julliard

BIG BANG

BIG BANG

I. Big Bang

Las galaxias parecen alejarse unas de otras a velocidades considerables. Las más lejanas huyen con la aceleración de doscientos treinta mil kilómetros por segundo, próxima a la de la luz.
El universo se hincha.
Asistimos al resultado de una gigantesca explosión.

II. Big Bang

Conociendo la distancia que separa las galaxias y la rapidez con que se alejan unas de otras, podemos, a través de cálculos, ir atrás en el tiempo, hasta principios de la expansión. De ahí que los partidarios de la teoría del *Big Bang* concluyan que el nacimiento del universo se produjo hace diez billones de años. "La evolución del mundo puede compararse con un grandioso fuego artificial cuyos últimos cohetes acaban de apagarse: quedan algunos residuos incandescentes, cenizas y humo. En las brasas más frías se extinguen soles." (Lemaître)

I. Big Bang

The galaxies appear to distance themselves one from the other at considerable velocities. The farthest ones flee, accelerating at two hundred thirty thousand kilometers a second, nearing the speed of light.
The universe swells.
We watch the emergence of a gigantic explosion.

II. Big Bang

Knowing the distance that separates galaxies and the speed with which they distance themselves, one from the other, we can, with calculation, go back in time, to the beginning of the expansion. From that point of view, those who believe in the Big Bang conclude that the birth of the universe was made manifest ten billion years ago. "The evolution of the world might be compared to grandiose fireworks whose final rockets have become extinguished: some residual incandescence remains, ashes and smoke. Suns are extinguished in the coldest of coals." (Lemaître)

III. Isomorfía

El astrónomo Americano Allan R. Sandage reveló, en el congreso de astrofísica que se desarrolla actualmente en Texas, que en junio de 1966 los astrónomos de Monte Palomar habían sido testigos de las más gigantescas de las explosiones de un objeto celeste jamás observada por el hombre. El objeto celeste de que se trata es un quasar que lleva el número 3C 446. Los quasars, descubiertos en 1963, pueden ser astros jóvenes, extremadamente lejanos—varios billones de años-luz—y muy luminosos. La explosión observada, que multiplicó por veinte la luminosidad del quasar 3C 446 pudo haberse producido hace algunos billones de años, tal vez poco después de la explosión inicial que, según la teoría del profesor Sandage, dio nacimiento al universo.

De la lucerna manchada, alta—contra los cristales el golpe de la arena—, la luz cae, cono mostaza.
La sombra del tubo de la ducha en la pared rosada.

En los baños del Hotel de la Confianza apareces, aguador desnudo.

(Afuera: sandalias arrastradas sobre el suelo cubierto de aserrín, la radio marroquí, y más lejos—jinetes que borra el resplandor naranja—, cascos, turbantes que se deshacen al viento.)

Rompes contra el suelo los cantarillos de agua podrida, te sacas el sexo, hules a oliva, te aprietas el glande, lo marcan tus dedos manchados de azafrán, de tintura púrpura.
La leche en la pared: punto denso, signo blanco que se dilata.
Un silencio.
Una risa.

Te pones la chilaba.
Yo, el impermeable.
(Afuera: el audio de la película: "Mañana, al alba, César atacará Alexia", y más lejos, el parpadeo del neón—"Luxor"—, el metro.)

                                                           Tiznit/Barbès-Rochechouart.

III. Isomorphism

The American astronomer Allan R. Sandage revealed, at the astrophysics conference that is taking place now in Texas, that in June, 1966 the astronomers of Mount Palomar witnessed the most gigantic explosions of a celestial object ever observed by man. The celestial object of note is a quasar that carries the number 3C 446. Quasars, discovered in 1963, can be young stars, extremely distant—various billions of light-years—and very luminous. The observed explosion, that multiplied by twenty the luminosity of the quasar 3C 446 could have occurred some billions of years ago, perhaps shortly after the initial explosion that, according to the theory of Professor Sandage, gave birth to the universe.

From the tarnished chandelier above—sand hitting the crystals,— light falls, a mustard cone.
The shadow of the shower pipe on the pink wall.

You appear in the baths of the Hotel de la Confianza, naked water seller.

(Outside: sandals dragged over the sawdust-covered ground, the Moroccan radio, and farther off—horsemen erased in orange radiance—, helmets, turbans undone in the wind.)

You break against the ground small pitchers of spoiled water, you take out your sex, smelling of olives, squeeze your gland, marking it with your fingers stained with saffron, with purple dye.
Milk on the wall: thick point, white sign dilating.
Silence.
Laughter.

You put on the djellaba.
I, my raincoat.
(Outside: sounds from a movie: "Tomorrow, at daybreak, Caesar will attack Alesia," and farther off, the blinking neon—"Luxor"—, the metro.

Tiznit/Barbès-Rochechouart.

IV. Hueco negro

Tradicionalmente, la deformación del espacio alrededor de un cuerpo masivo se compara con la de una membrana de caucho horizontal bajo el peso de una bola. Cuando un derrumbe gravitacional se produce, asistimos al nacimiento de un verdadero hueco en el espacio-tiempo, hueco que devora totalmente la materia del objeto. Es la geometría misma del espacio-tiempo lo que, en una cierta zona, se ve arrastrado por el derrumbe. Toda materia todo rayo proyectado a partir de esa zona, es capturado irreversiblemente y no puede escapar. De modo que, del objeto derrumbado no puede llegarnos ninguna señal. Un fotón que tratara de emerger de él encontraría en la situación de un niño tratando de subir a la carrera una escalera mecánica que bajara a gran velocidad. La velocidad del fotón hacia el exterior será siempre inferior a la de la *implosión*: la luz quedará irremediablemente atrapada. Queda pues explicado por qué a esos objetos celestes que han llegado a fases extremas de su derrumbe gravitacional se ha llamado "huecos negros."

Arena aspirada en las aristas: los objetos van perdiendo sus bordes, redondeando sus ángulos, piedras gastadas.
El polvo que los vacía traza las diagonales del cubo, desaparece en el centro del hueco.
De las paredes se desprende la cal roja; del suelo, fibras de madera; el tapiz se desteje.

Colores roídes.
Poros.
Superficies que el iris devora.

Planos cerrándose.
Vertientes blanqueadas.

El rumor de la erosión me duerme.

IV. Black Hole

Traditionally, the deformation of space around a massive body is compared to a horizontal rubber membrane beneath the weight of a ball. When a gravitational collapse is produced, we witness the birth of a true hole in spacetime, a hole which devours totally the object's material. It is the very geometry of spacetime that, in a certain zone, is seen dragged through the collapse. All material, every ray projected from this zone, is captured irreversibly and cannot escape. Such that, no sign of the collapsed object will reach us. A photon that might attempt to emerge from it will find itself in the situation of a child trying to hurriedly climb up an escalator that is descending at a rapid velocity. The velocity of the photon headed outward will always be inferior to that of the *implosion*: the light will remain irremediably trapped. Herein is explained why those celestial objects that have garnered extreme levels of gravitational pull are called "black holes."

Sand blown around the edges: the objects begin to lose their borders, rounding their angles, spent stones.
Dust emptied out of them traces the cube's diagonals, disappears in the open space.
Red lime detaches from the walls; from the floor, fibers of wood; the tapestry goes undone.

Gnawed colors.
Pores.
Surfaces that the iris devours.

Closing planes.
Whitened slopes.

The erosion's murmurs put me to sleep.

V. Cangrejo

Desde hace algunos años la nebulosa del Cangrejo era conocida como fuente de rayos X, pero el descubrimiento del pulsar óptico del Cangrejo, en 1968, llevó a H. Friedmann, del Naval Research Laboratory, a un nuevo análisis de de sus resultados. El astrónomo encontró que un nueve por ciento del flujo X de la nebulosa se emitía en forma de pulsaciones. La energía de cada pulsación es equivalente a la que nuestra civilización pudiera producir, en forma de electricidad, durante diez millones de años.

Muros de amuletos, lámparas encendidas: elipses lentas.
A través de los cristales paralelos, cubiertos de pulseras, entre piedras brutales, se abren prismadas franjas verdes, plata de un paño.
Turbante, greñas quemadas; ante los ojos dos aros de oro: el humo del té los empaña.

Detrás de los collares sacudidos, del martilleo de las monedas, pinzas quebradas, en el platillo cae el cangrejo:
té en el tapiz
leche en el espejo
astillas rojas de carapacho
en las alhajas coágulos blancos.

V. Crab

Some years ago, the Crab Nebula was known to be a source of x-rays, but the discovery of the Crab pulsar in 1968, led H. Friedmann, at the Naval Research Laboratory, to perform a new analysis of his results. The astronomer found that nine percent of the x-rays flowing from the nebula were emitted in the form of pulsations. The energy from each pulse is equivalent to that which our civilization might produce, in electrical form, in ten million years.

Walls covered in amulets, lit lamps: slow ellipses.
Through the parallel crystals, covered in bracelets, between brutal stones, open green borders of prisms, silver of a cloth.
Turban, burnt tangled hair; against the eyes two rings of gold: the tea's fumes cover them in mist.

Behind shaken necklaces, the hammering of coins, broken pliers, a crab falls onto the plate:
  tea on the tapestry
  milk on the mirror
  red splinters from a shell
  white clots on the jewels.

VI. Luz fósil

Así, los astrónomos tratan de explicar por qué el flujo de rayos X procedente del universo parece entre diez y cien veces superior a la suma de los flujos de todas las galaxias reunidas. ¿No habrán detectado aún todas las galaxias que emiten rayos X? ¿O se trata de una irradiación difusa, testigo de la explosión que dio origen al universo?

Medir sus reflejos en la arista de un pez,
en el ojo de cocuyo,
en la sura de la sombra del dátil;

comparar la cal del marabuto
con el paño de un monje mercedario,

con la nieve bajo el antílope
la sal de la garza fósil,

con el semen
la Vía Láctea.

VI. Fossilized Light

In this way, astronomers attempt to explain why the universe's emission of x-rays appears to be between ten and one hundred times greater than the sum of those emitted from all galaxies. Have they yet detected all galaxies that emit x-rays? Or does this concern a diffuse irradiation, testimony to the explosion that gave birth to the universe?

To measure its reflections on the edge of a fish,
in the firefly's eye,
in the sura of the finger's shadow;

compare the marabout's lime
with the Mercedarian monk's cloth,

with the snow beneath an antelope
the salt of a fossilized heron,

with semen,
the Milky Way.

XII. Cuerpo divino

El peso de tu cuerpo
sobre mi cuerpo
piel sutura cifrada
saliva Verde
sobre la espalda
vértebra entre vértebra
piernas anudadas
untadas la laca fosforescente
los huesos
iluminan la habitación de muros negros
volúmenes articulándose
s'emboîtant
entrando
en silencio
aceitados
lentamente
unos en otros
unos en otros
resplandor
que desciende
por el muro
a lo largo del muro,
astros muertos cayendo
hasta el mármol
de la sábana.

XII. Heavenly Body

The weight of your body
on my body
suturing skin ciphered
Green saliva
on your back
spine on spine
knees knotted
smeared with phosphorescent lacquer
the bones
light up the black-walled room
volumes articulating
s'emboîtant
entering
in silence
greased
slowly
each in another
each in another
radiance
descending
over the wall
along the distance of the wall,
dead asters falling
to the sheet's
marble.

OTROS POEMAS

OTHER POEMS

Sexteto habanero

Ainsi le bon temps regrettons
Entre nous, pauvres vieilles sottes,
Assises bas, à croupetons,
Tout en un tas comme pelotes,
A petit feu de chenevottes,
Tôt allumées, tôt éteintes;
Et jadis fûmes si mignottes!
Ainsi en prend à maints et maintes.

François Villon, *Les Regrets de la Belle Heaumière*

I

¿Qué se hicieron los cantantes,
los reyes, los Matamoros
de dril nevado y los oros
de las barajas de antes?
¿Quién las tardes del Cervantes
recuerda, y aquel grabado
del Diario, desdibujado,
y los bailables de Sagua?

(Las guitarras llenas de agua
están, y el tambor rajado.)

II

Tu nombre, Elegua,
para abrir, para
cerrar la puerta.
La Puerta:
esplenden las ofrendas, oro,
espacio ardiente.

Havana Sextet

Ainsi le bon temps regrettons
Entre nous, pauvres vieilles sottes,
Assises bas, à croupetons,
Tout en un tas comme pelotes,
A petit feu de chenevottes,
Tôt allumées, tôt éteintes;
Et jadis fûmes si mignottes!
Ainsi en prend à maints et maintes.

François Villon, *Les Regrets de la Belle Heaumière*

I

What's become of the singers,
the kings, the Matamoros
of snow-covered drill and the gold
on the old decks of cards?
Who in the Cervantine afternoons
remembers? And that long-lost print
of the *Diario*, faded,
and the dancing in Sagua?

(The guitars are full
of water, and the drum is ripped open.)

II

Your name, Elegua,
to open, to
close the gate.
The Gate:
the offerings glisten, gold,
burning space.

III

Aquellos barriletes y el coronel de Las Marías
zumbando como un loco y tocando la luna.

Del baile y Marquesano y la conga no quedan
ni la persiana el abre y el asómate.
Tomaron la cerveza en los clarines
y el bailador de Macorina estaba.
No han venido la China ni la "ojitos
de piñata." Flauta de canutillo, chacumbele.

Ya de aquí no nos vamos.

IV

¿Los dioses
se fueron, se quedaron,
murieron con Beny Moré
ellos que con él se alucinaban,
o habitan aún las orquestas habaneras,
las trompetas como dos lluvias de flechas,
los cascabeles roncos,
y las tardes de músicos y monos?

III

Those clarinets and the colonel from Las Marías
humming like a mad man and playing the moon.

Nothing remains of the dance and the Marquesano
and the conga, not even the curtain, its opening, and the reveal.
They drank beer in bugles
and the dancer of Macorina was there.
Neither the Chinese woman nor the one with "piñata
eyes" have come. Small reed flute, Chacumbele.

We will not leave here anymore.

IV

Did the gods
leave, stay,
die with Beny Moré
those who hallucinated with him,
or do they still haunt the Havana orchestras,
the trumpets like two showers of arrows,
the hoarse rattles,
and the afternoons of musicians and handsome men?

V

"¿De dónde serán,
serán de Santiago
tierra soberana?"—preguntaban
por ferias y verbenas.

(Oigo aún aquellas voces,
la mesa electoral,
mis padres bailando.)

El de sus leontinas,
oro empañado,
fue el de la tarde.

VI

El día es cegador,
la noche una humedad morada.
Girar como trompos los ahorcados
—ojos abiertos,
rostros pintarrajeados—.

No te asombres cuando veas
al alacrán tumbando caña.

V

"Where are they from,
 from Santiago,
 the sovereign land?" they would ask
at fairs and outside dances.

(I hear even now the voices,
the electoral table,
my parents dancing.)

The man of watch chains,
faded gold,
he was there in the afternoon.

VI

Day is blinding,
night a purple humidity.
The hanging men turn like spinning tops
—open eyes,
faces smeared—.

Do not be afraid when you see
the scorpion cutting down the cane.

Páginas en blanco (Cuadros de Franz Kline)

I *wax wing*

No hay silencio
sino
cuando el Otro
habla
(Blanco no:
colores que se escapan
por los bordes).
Ahora
que el poema está escrito.
La página vacía.

II *shenandoah wall*

La pared cruje.
Grieta en lo blanco.
Allá va, desunido,
el cuarto.
Detrás del tragaluz
un rostro, otro,
mirándose,
mirándonos.

Blank Pages (Paintings by Franz Kline)

    I *wax wing*

There is no silence
but
when the Other
speaks
(White no:
colors that escape
beyond the edges.)
Now
that the poem is written.
The page blank.

    II *shenandoah wall*

The wall creaks.
Crack in the white.
There it goes, undone,
the bedroom.
Behind the skylight
a face, another,
looking at itself
looking at us.

III *étude pour crow dancer*

Un cubo despegado.
Pegada la oreja a la pared.
Oye.
Algo va a romperse. Algo
crece.
Lo que en el muro
      hierve.

IV *harley red*

El sueño no:
la pérdida.
El blanco roedor,
que ciega.
Pierdo pie. Todo es compuerta.
Mira:
el muro sangra.

III *étude pour crow dancer*

A cube unstuck.
The ear fixed to the wall.
Listen.
Something is going to break. Something
grows.
Something in the wall
    boils.

IV *harley red*

Not the dream:
its loss.
The gnawing white;
that blinds.
I lose foot. Everything a floodgate.
Look:
the wall bleeds.

V   *zinc door*

Abierta no,
entrejunta.
Esa ranura mira.
Detrás de lo blanco,
blanco.
Ahora el silencio.
Las paredes se cuartean.
El cuarto desmoronado,
navega. Y ese brillo.
La puerta transparente.

VI   *black and white*

La raya negra y el battello,
el monte siamo tutti,
el barco blanco sobre el agua blanca
y la fijeza
de los pájaros sobre la Salute.
Pase,
Il fait beau del otro lado
del otro lado, digo,
del río.
       Estamos todos.

V *zinc door*

Open no,
half-closed.
That keyhole watches.
Behind the white,
white.
Now silence.
The walls are divided.
The room collapsed,
sails. And that brilliance.
The transparent door.

VI *black and white*

The black line and the boat,
the hill *siamo tutti*,
the white boat on white water
the stillness
of birds on the Salute.
Pass over,
Il fait beau on the other side
on the other side, I mean,
of the river.
      We're all here.

Pavo real de Carlo Crivelli

Barcas vacías
bajando
por canales blancos:
los muchachos
—zapatos altos,
pelo rubio lacio—
por los corredores
de arena
inclinados.
Entre jaulas
donde aletean
miedosos de Döng
—vuelos oblicuos—
faisanes.

Carlo Crivelli's Peacock

Empty rowboats
go down
white canals:
the young men
—high shoes,
blond straight hair—
through the sloped
passageways
of sand.
In cages
where they flap their wings
afraid of Döng
—oblique flights—
pheasants.

Cubos de Larry Bell

cubo
de vidrio
polvo
de metal

reflejo
ahumado:
versión
del sol

(eco
de
cobre)

arista
cara irisada
sitar

Cubes by Larry Bell

glass
cube
metal
dust

smoky
reflection:
version
of the sun

(echo
of
copper)

edge
iridescent face
sitar

Inter femora

Lúbrica hada
a dolor ida
metida
sacada

con cuidado
con K.
Y.

de lado
...sí:
¡ay!

                        Mete!
Y si ardor o pudor o amor ay, saca!
Lamida maruga, mojada matraca
entra mejor. Si en este brete
                se te
cae, recobra su natura de estaca:
hueso embadurnado de laca,
de perro mascado tolete.

Foutez allègrement! La vida es eso:
darle hasta que se caiga a la sin hueso
untada con "K.Y." (sabor menta).

Considerar sin fin el fin de cuenta:
uñas y pelo y sobre la osamenta,
blanda corona, derramado el seso.

Inter Femora

Lube it, fairy
pained
penetrated
taken out

with care
with K.
Y.

from the side
... sí:
¡ay!

                    Put it in!
And if there's burning, modesty, or love, take it out!
Licked rattle, wet noise-maker
enters better. If in this fix
                 you
fall, recover your stake's nature:
bone smeared in lacquer,
dog mulling over dick.

Foutez allègrement! Life's like this:
give it all until it falls boneless
smeared in K.Y. (mint flavored).

Consider endlessly the end of the count:
fingernails and hair and over the skeleton
a tender crown, the senses spilled out.

UN TESTIGO FUGAZ Y DISFRAZADO

(1985)

A FLEETING AND MASKED WITNESS

(1985)

La transparente luz del mediodía
filtraba por los bordes paralelos
de la ventana, y el contorno de los
frutos—o el de tu piel—resplandecía.

El sopor de la siesta: lejanía
de la isla. En el cambiante cielo
crepuscular, o en el opaco velo
ante el rojo y naranja aparecía

otro fulgor, otro fulgor. Dormía
en una casa litoral y pobre:
en el aire las lámparas de cobre

trazaban lentas espirales sobre
el blanco mantel, sombra que urdía
el teorema de la otra geometría.

The transparent light at midday
filtered through the window's parallel
borders, and the outline of fruits—
or of your skin—shone.

Slumber of siesta: distance
of the island. In the turbulent twilit
sky or in the opaque veil
before the red and orange, came

another glow, another glow. Sleeping
in a humble seaside home:
copper lamps

traced slow spirals in the air
over the white tablecloth, shadows casting
the theorem of that other geometry.

El rumor de las máquinas crecía
en la sala contigua: ya mi espera
de un adjetivo—o de tu cuerpo—no era
más que un intento de acortar el día.

La noche que llegaba y precedía
el viento del desierto, la certera
luz—o tus pies desnudos en la estera—
del ocaso, su tiempo suspendía.

No recuerdo el amor sino el deseo;
no la falta de fe, sino la esfera—
imagen confrontando su espejeo

con la textura blanca, verdadera
página—o tu cuerpo que aún releo—:
vasto ideograma de la primavera.

The murmur of machines was growing
in the adjacent room: already my hope
for an adjective—or for your body—was nothing
more than an attempt to shorten the day.

The night that was arriving and preceding
the desert wind, the certain
light—or your naked feet on the mat—
of sunset, was suspending time.

I do not remember love, only desire;
not the lack of faith, only the sphere—
the image facing its reflection

with white texture, the true
page—or your body, which I still reread—:
vast ideogram of spring.

Ni la voz precedida por el eco,
ni el reflejo voraz de los desnudos
cuerpos en el azogue de los mudos
cristales, sino el trazo escueto, seco:

las frutas en la mesa y el paisaje
colonial. Cuando el tiempo de la siesta
nos envolvía en lo denso de su oleaje,
o en el rumor de su apagada fiesta,

cuando de uno en el otro se extinguía
la sed, cuando avanzaba por la huerta
la luz que el flamboyant enrojecía,

abríamos entonces la gran puerta
al rumor insular del mediodía
y a la puntual naturaleza muerta.

Not the voice preceded by the echo,
nor the ravenous reflection of the naked
bodies in the quicksilver of the quiet
crystals, but the simple brushstroke, dry:

the fruits on the table and the colonial
landscape. When the hour of the siesta
enveloped us in the density of its swelling seas,
or in the murmur of its ended fiesta,

when one in the other extinguished
thirst, when light advanced
through the orchard that the flame tree reddened,

we opened then the great door
to the insular murmur of noon
and to the timely still life.

Omítemela más, que lo omitido
cuando alcanza y define su aporía
enciende en el reverso de su día
un planeta en la noche del sentido.

A pulso no: que no disfruta herido,
por flecha berniana o por manía
de brusquedad, el templo humedecido
(de Venus, el segundo). Ya algún día

lubricantes o medios naturales
pondrás entre los bordes con taimada
prudencia, o con cautela ensalivada

que atenúen la quema de tu entrada:
pues de amor y de ardor en los anales
de la historia la nupcia está cifrada.

Pull out of me more than what was left out:
for when reaching and defining aporia
a planet on the other side of its day
ignites in the night of its senses.

Not by force: for the humid temple
(of Venus, the second) does not take pleasure
in being wounded by the Berninian arrow
or by frenzy. Someday you will lay

lubricants or natural substances
between the borders with cunning
prudence, or with salivated caution

that might ease the burning of your entrance:
because with love and with ardor in the annals
of history our nuptials are ciphered.

Entrando en ti, cabeza con cabeza,
pelo con pelo, boca contra boca:
el aire que respiras—la fijeza
del recuerdo—, respiro, y en la poca

luz de la tarde—rayo que no cesa
entre los huesos abrasados—toca
los bordes de tu cuerpo: luz que apresa
la forma. Ya su cénit la convoca

a otro vacío donde su blancura
borra, marca de arena, tu figura.
El día devorado de sonidos

quema, de trecho en trecho, su espesura
y vuelca de ceniza la textura
en la noche voraz de los sentidos.

Entering you, head to head,
hair to hair, mouth against mouth:
the air you breathe—fixation
of the memory—, I breathe, and the slight

light of evening—ray that does not cease
among the burning bones—touches
your body's borders: light imprisons
form. Already evening's zenith calls

to it another void where the white of light
erases, a mark in sand, your figure.
The day devoured in sounds

burns, from distance to distance, its thickness
and turns its texture to ash
in the ravenous night of the senses.

El émbolo brillante y engrasado
embiste jubiloso la ranura
y derrama su blanca quemadura
más abrasante cuanto más pausado.

Un testigo fugaz y disfrazado
ensaliva y escruta la abertura
que el volumen dilata y que sutura
su propia lava. Y en el ovalado

mercurio tangencial sobre la alfombra
(la torre, embadurnada penetrando,
chorreando de su miel, saliendo, entrando)

descifra el ideograma de la sombra:
el pensamiento es ilusión: templando
viene despacio la que no se nombra.

Glittering, greased, the piston
charges joyfully at the opening
and spills its white burn,
scorching more the less hurried it is.

A fleeting and masked witness
spits on and probes the opening
which dilates with volume and sutures
its own lava. And in the oval

mercury tangential to the carpet
(the tower, smeared penetrating,
dripping of its honey, leaving, entering)

deciphers the ideogram of the shadow:
thought is illusion: cooling down
that which has no name comes slow.

Aunque ungiste el umbral y ensalivaste
no pudo penetrar, lamida y suave,
ni siquiera calar tan vasta nave,
por su volumen como por su lastre.

Burlada mi cautela y en contraste
—linimentos, pudores ni cuidados—
con exiguos anales olvidados
de golpe y sin aviso te adentraste.

Nunca más tolerancia ni acogida
hallará en mí tan solapada inerte
que a placeres antípodas convida

y en rigores simétricos se invierte:
muerte que forma parte de la vida.
Vida que forma parte de la muerte.

Though you anointed and wet the threshold
with spit, you could not penetrate, licked and soft,
not even submerge, so vast a ship,
its volume and its ballast.

My prudence teased and with yours against me
—lacking liniments, modesty, or cares—
with exiguous forgotten annals
suddenly and without warning you entered.

There will never be more submission in me
or welcome, so laid down and still,
than when I'm given to antipodal pleasures

and inverted in symmetrical rigors:
death that forms part of life.
Life that forms part of death.

Si marrona cedió, si abandonóme
ya adentrado el trajín, si presentada
—hyalo-miel sobre cúpula frotada—
al umbral deseoso y tibio no me

respondió, si flaqueó, quedó contrita
ante el abierto lapso lubricado,
si de frente embistió, mas no de lado,
habrá que perdonarla por su cuita.

No se le inculpe por tamña treta
si vejada quedó más que ceñida
y ante el umbral exiguo fue discreta.

Golpetazos como ése da la vida.
O la muerte, que es diestra y más secreta,
y en su inmóvil golpear nunca te olvida.

If it darkened, if it abandoned me,
already deep in the coming and going, if presented
—honey over the massaged cupola—
before the anxious and warm threshold it did not

respond to me, if faltering, it became contrite
before the open, lubricated lapse,
if it attacked head on, not from the side,
one would have to forgive it for its affliction.

Do not blame it for its feint size
if it was left humiliated rather than tight-fitting,
if it became discreet against my meagre threshold.

Life gives blows like this.
Or death, which is deft and more secretive
and in its motionless blow never forgets you.

Renuncia a tu cuidado, bien lo sé: tras
ese dolor que tu embestida aqueja,
en alivio y placer muda la queja,
más sosegada cuanto más penetras.

Cerveza transmutada o sidra añeja,
del oro tibio la furiosa recta
su apagado licor suma y proyecta
sobre el cuerpo deseoso que festeja

tanto derrame. A bálsamos o ardides
que atenúen la quema de tu entrada
nunca recurras. Mientras menos cuides,

unjas, prevengas, o envaselinada
disimules, mejor. Para que olvides
el mudo simulacro de la nada.

Let go, I know this well: behind
each pain your attack exacts,
my plaint is muted in relief and delight,
the more hushed the deeper you drive.

Beer transmuted or aged cider,
with heated gold the frantic thing, upright,
gathers and casts its muffled elixir
over the longing body, lauding

so much flow. Never go
to balms or cons to calm the burning
of your entrance. The less you fear,

embalm, fend off, or conceal
in salves, the better. Thus may you forget
the silent simulacrum of death.

A Gerardo Mello-Mourão

El paso no, del dios, sino la huella
escrita entre las líneas de la piedra
verdinegra y porosa. Aún la hiedra
retiene las pisadas, aún destella

de su cuerpo el contorno sobre rojos
sanguíneos o vinosos: en los vasos
fragmentados, dispersos. No los pasos
del dios, sino las huellas; no los ojos:

la mirada. Ni el texto, ni la trama
de la voz, sino el mar que los decanta.
En su tumba—las islas ideograma

de esa página móvil donde tanta
frase, no bien grabada, se derrama—,
sumergida, tu estatua ciega, canta.

To Gerardo Mello-Mourão

Not the footstep of the god, but the footprint
written between the dark-green and porous
lines in the stone. Still the ivy
preserves his footsteps, still the contour

of his body gleams over the sanguineous
and wine-colored reds: in the broken,
scattered glasses. Not the footsteps
of the god, but the footprints; not the eyes:

the gaze. Not the text, not the plot
of the voice, but the ocean that decants them.
In his tomb—the islands, ideogram

of this moveable page where so many
words, not well recorded, spill—
submerged, your blind statue, sings.

A Octavio Paz

Las húmedas terrazas dominaban
el templo, la planicie entre dos mares,
superpuestas, azules, triangulares.
Simétricas estatuas deslizaban

sus fragmentos de mármol por la nieve
—fueron torsos de Apolo, manos anchas
que el musgo ha devorado con sus manchas—
fresca, trazando un laberinto breve.

Los cuerpos arrastrados por el río
han quedado en la arena sepultados
bajo las piedras nítidas del lecho.

En el delta una mano, el globo frío
de unos ojos han sido rescatados.
Y más allá una frente, un brazo, el pecho.

To Octavio Paz

The humid balconies overlooked
the temple, the plain between two seas,
superimposed, blue, triangular.
Symmetrical statues slipped

their fragments of marble through the snow
—torsos of Apollo, wide hands
the moss had devoured in its stains—
cool, tracing a brief labyrinth.

The bodies dragged by the river
remain buried in the sand
below the clean bed of stones.

In the delta, a hand, the cold globe
of some eyes that have been salvaged.
And beyond that a forehead, an arm, the chest.

Página de un diario

Pasado, todo el día, en el complejo
trámite funerario. No es la muerte
lo que derrumba con su hachazo —fuerte
así es el hombre—, sino el turbio espejo

que nos tiende. Si su mercurio muestra
tetanizada de dolor y miedo
una cara deforme o el remedo
de una cara —un borrón—: eso es la nuestra

devuelta a su verdad por la guadaña
que no ahuyenta la fuerza ni la maña.
En su brasa te alumbres o te quemes,

que no sepa, ni en sombra, lo que temes,
ese dios que veneras y encareces.
Porque eso mismo te dará. Y con creces.

Page from a Diary

Gone, all day, in the complex
funereal procedures. It isn't death
that devastates with its blow—we
in this way are strong—, but the turbid mirror

he hands us. If his mercury reveals,
a face deformed, tightened in pain
and fear, or the false reflection
of a face—rough smudge—: that is ours

returned to its truth by the scythe
that neither strength nor skill can turn away from.
In his ember, you cast light or you burn,

not knowing, not even in shadow, what you fear,
that god you revere and exhort.
Because that is what he will give you. And more.

Ahora la muerte lo ha ganado todo:
los cuadernos, los muebles de madera,
los cobres empañados y la espera,
que es una de sus formas y su modo

de aparecer. Si llega paso a paso
sorprende en el amor o en el trabajo
y apresura el jadeo con su tajo
o arranca al laborioso de un zarpazo;

si adelanta, solícita, su día
y te llama, simula indiferencia.
Reconoce su tosca alegoría

en todo lo que cae, en la consciencia
que se apaga. Si pasa, desconfía.
De nada sirve tu saber. Paciencia.

Now death has taken everything:
notebooks, wooden furniture,
tarnished copper and the waiting,
which is one of his forms and his way

of appearing. If he arrives step by step
he takes one by surprise in love or at work
and hastens one's panting with a slash
or uproots the worker with a lash;

If, solicitous, he hurries his day
and calls you, feign indifference.
See his coarse allegory

in all that befalls you, in your consciousness
going dim. If he passes, beware.
Knowledge helps nothing. Patience.

Perdido, el Poderoso se va huyendo
de la revolución y de la quema.
Dos noches sobre el mar vela y blasfema
y contempla las cúpulas ardiendo.

En la tercera noche ya se sueña
flanqueado por extraños animales
que con flautas doradas dan la seña
de su entrada a los círculos glaciales del país enemigo.

Danza y bebe
invocando el festejo de la nieve;
dibuja sobre el agua con la daga

un castillo de muros congelados
que, junto con la nave, el mar se traga.
En la noche de almejas y de ahogados.

Vanquished, the Powerful One flees
revolution and burning.
For two nights, at sea, he holds vigil and curses
and contemplates the smoldering cupulas.

On the third night, he finally dreams
flanked by strange animals
that, with gilded flutes, signal
his entrance to the glacial circles of his enemy country.

He dances and drinks
invoking festivities of snow;
with his dagger, he draws on water

a castle of frozen walls
that, with his ship, the sea swallows.
In the night of clams and drowned men.

Pido la canonización de Virgilio Piñera

Poco interés presentan estas cosas
para un Concilio, que otras más urgentes
—la talla de los ángeles, las fuentes
del Edén—, y sin duda, más valiosas

apremian sin cesar. Insisto empero
para que tenga sitio en los altares
este mártir de arenas insulares.
Por textual, su milagro verdadero

dio presa fácil a los cabecillas
y a los sarcasmos que, de tanto en tanto,
interrumpen las furias amarillas,

las madres del exilio y del espanto.
Es por eso que a Roma, y de rodillas,
iré a exigir que lo proclamen santo.

Requesting the Canonization of Virgilio Piñera

Such things are of little interest to a Council
compared to others more urgent and, without a doubt,
more valuable, hurrying them ceaselessly—the stature
of angels, the founts of Eden.

I insist however
that there be space on the altars
for this martyr of insular beaches.
With text, his true miracle,

he easily imprisoned the ringleaders
and their sneers that, now and then,
cut short the yellow Furies,

the mothers of exile and fright.
For this reason I'll go to Rome on my knees,
to beg that they proclaim him saint.

Al Buda de Chinatown

Entre frutas doradas como esferas,
fénix, dragones, ideograma breve,
sobre un biombo empañado por la nieve,
paciente Sakiamuni, oras y esperas

en exilio. Quemaron las banderas
de plegaria, los mantos amarillos;
garabatearon hoces y martillos
y mancharon con armas las esteras.

Cuños de lacre rojo, un pergamino:
en un templo interior del barrio chino,
bajo un neón—árbol intermitente

de la Bodi—, Gautama, el ascendente
leopardo cuyo rostro es el camino
de una galaxia sobre el occidente.

To the Buddha of Chinatown

Among fruits gilded as suns,
phoenix, dragons, a brief ideogram,
over a folding screen coated in snow,
patient Sakyamuni, you pray and wait

in exile. They burned your prayer
flags, yellow cloaks;
they scribbled sickles and hammers
on your mats and stained them with guns.

Stamps of red lacquer, a parchment:
in an interior temple of Chinatown,
beneath a neon light—intermittent tree

of Bodhi—Gautama, the ascendant
leopard whose face is the path
of a galaxy over the west.

A Luce López-Baralt

No por azar, por gusto del dislate,
ni por obedecer a una figura,
habló de una cegante noche oscura.
Que toda exaltación o disparate

aparente, se indague, y no se ciña
—el lenguaje no basta— a un simple juego:
de granadas y lámparas de fuego
bebió un vino, de antes de la viña.

No percibió ni forma ni sonido,
mas con la sangre lo irrigó un sentido
ajeno a la palabra y a la imagen.

Dejemos, de esa heráldica, que viajen
los símbolos, el mudo abecedario:
agua y sed, brasa y luz, cuerpo y sudario.

To Luce López-Baralt

Not by chance, for love of nonsense,
or to obey a figure,
he spoke from a blinding black night.
That all exaltation or apparent

folly be investigated and not girded
—language is not enough—to a simple game:
before the days of vineyards, he drank wine
made from pomegranates in lamps of fire.

He did not perceive form or sound,
but with blood he fed a foreign
sense in the word and the image.

May it be, from this heraldry, that symbols
move, the silent alphabet:
water and thirst, ember and light, body and shroud.

Morandi

Una lámpara. Un vaso. Una botella.
Sin más utilidad ni pertenencia
que estar ahí, que dar a la consciencia
un soporte casual. Mas no la huella

del hombre que la enciende o que los usa
para beber: todo ha sido blanqueado
o cubierto de cal y nada acusa
abandono, descuido ni cuidado.

Sólo la luz es familiar y escueta,
el relieve eficaz; la sombra neta
se alarga en el mantel. El día quedo

sigue el paso del tiempo con su vaga
irrealidad. La tarde ya se apaga.
Los objetos se abrazan: tienen miedo.

Morandi

A lamp. A glass. A bottle.
No more utility or pertinence
than being there, than bringing to mind
casual support. But not a trace

of the man who lights the lamp or drinks from
the glass, the bottle: everything has been whitened
or covered with lime and nothing reveals
abandon, negligence, or care.

Only light is familiar and unadorned,
the relief efficient; the true shadow
grows over the tablecloth. The quiet day

follows the passage of time with its vague
illusion. Now afternoon comes to an end.
The objects embrace each other: afraid.

Rothko

A Andrés Sánchez Robayna

No los colores, ni la forma pura.
Memoria de la tinta. Sedimento
que decanta la luz de su pigmento,
más allá de la tela y su armadura.

Las líneas no, ni sombra ni textura,
ni la breve ilusión del movimiento;
nada más que el silencio: el sentimiento
de estar en su presencia. La Pintura

en franjas paralelas cuya bruma
cruza la tela intacta, aunque teñida
de cinabrio, de vino que se esfuma;

púrpura, bermellón, anaranjada...
El rojo de la sangre derramada
selló su exploración. También su vida.

Rothko

To Andrés Sánchez Robayna

Not the colors, or the pure form.
Memory of ink. Sediment
that decants light from its pigment,
beyond the canvas and its framework.

Not the lines, not the shadow or texture,
not the brief illusion of movement;
nothing more than silence: the feeling
of being in its presence. The Painting

between parallel borders whose mist
crosses the intact canvas, though tinged
with cinnabar, with wine that fades;

purple, vermillion, orange...
The red of spilled blood
sealed his exploration. Also his life.

UN TESTIGO PERENNE Y DELATADO

(1993)

A PERENNIAL AND BETRAYED WITNESS

(1993)

SONETOS

SONNETS

San Juan de la Cruz

Levitaste convulso, al traste diste
con cilicio, sotana y relicario,
concluyendo los diálogos que a diario,
más que con frases, con amor tuviste.

De la testa a los pies, un traqueteo.
La boca de salitre sin aliento.
Un no sé qué te socavó el cimiento,
vecino del desmayo y del mareo.

El alma liberada de su cargo:
toda imprenta del cuerpo; todo lazo
desatado en los nervios; seco el hueso.

No se sabe qué fue ni si fue largo
ese dejar de ser. Brusco zarpazo
de lo absoluto: la fusión con eso.

Saint John of the Cross

Trembling, you rose, discarded
your cilice, cassock, and reliquary,
concluding the dialogues that daily,
more than with words, you had with love.

From head to toe, a clattering.
The mouth, a breathless saltpeter.
An unknown thing cut the ground from beneath you,
neighbor of blackout and vertigo.

The soul freed of its charge:
all the body's traces; all knot
unbound at the nerve; the bone, dry.

We do not know what took place or if it was long
this leaving of being. Sudden lash
of the absolute: and with it his union.

Santa Teresa de Ávila

A Elizabeth Burgos

Dios te perdone, Juan de la Miseria,
que la pintaste legañosa y fea,
y perdone también a quien la vea
bajo este ruin disfraz de la materia

y no bajo el de un ángel abrasado
que otro ángel, por amor, flecha y castiga.
—No hay nada que se piense o que se diga
más hondo que este amor y su cuidado—.

El reino recorrió diseminado
no la revolución, mas la reforma
radical, sin violencia—siempre y cuando

fuera posible—. Aunque maltrechos sobre
los caminos, sus pies fueron la norma.
De andar y desandar. De andar, la pobre.

Saint Teresa of Ávila

To Elizabeth Burgos

God forgive you, Juan de la Miseria,
because you painted her tired and ugly,
and forgive whoever sees her
beneath that wicked material disguise

and not beneath a burnt angel's
which another angel, for love, pierces and punishes.
—There is nothing thought or spoken
deeper than such love and its care—.

Her reign made known
not revolution, but radical
reformation without violence—always and whenever

possible—. Although wretched
on the streets, her feet were the norm.
Moving forward and coming back. Moving forward, poor thing.

Lucidez

Jorge Luis Borges

De cuantos hombres Dios ha reclamado
a su diestra, ninguno tan preciso
en su misión: la de nombrar lo que hizo
el Creador torpe y apresurado.

Necesitaba el Hacedor supremo
de un humano hacedor, austral y ciego,
que completara su invención: un juego
de sílabas ardientes, que al extremo

de su caída en el vacío adverso,
se decantan en forma de universo.
Supo soñarlas el Demiurgo altivo,

darles textura, resonancia, nombre
—y su imagen, entre ellas, dar al hombre—.
Pero aún le faltaba un adjetivo.

Clarity

Jorge Luis Borges

Of all the men God called
to his right hand, none was as precise
in his mission: to name what the Creator
had clumsily and hastily made.

The supreme Maker was in need
of a human maker, austral and blind,
to complete his invention: a game
of ardent syllables that, to the far end

of their fall through the adverse void,
are decanted in the form of a universe.
He learned how to dream in them the burning Demiurge,

give them texture, resonance, name
—and give his image, among them, to man—.
But even then he lacked an adjective.

Alegoría de Holbein

Un testigo perenne y delatado,
depuesto ya el disfraz y la ceguera
simulada, se entrega. Lo que espera
revela su dibujo de costado.

De frente es garabato alambicado,
hueso de jibia, nave estrafalaria
que enseña su figura funeraria
al que se va despacio y descuidado.

El cartílago seca y resquebraja
bailando al son de la orquestica muda
sin fanfarria que anuncie los conciertos.

Flores letales tejen su mortaja.
La granizada fue de azufre. Y ruda
la danza de los vivos y los muertos.

Allegory by Holbein

A perennial and betrayed witness,
his mask already fallen and his blindness
feigned, turns himself in. What awaits
is revealed in the drawing of his profile.

Head-on, he's an elaborate scribble,
bone of cuttlefish, lavish ship
disclosing his funereal figure
to those who pass slowly off guard.

His cartilage dries and cracks
dancing to the tune of the mute orchestra
without fanfare announcing concerts.

Lethal flowers weave their shroud.
The hailstorm was of sulphur. And rough
was the dance of the living and the dead.

Para el árbol de "La Recoleta"

¡Qué lección para el hombre: proliferas
en todos los sentidos! En el viento
son tus ramas emblema y argumento
de toda plenitud. O las banderas

de una plegaria. No comienza el día
sin que pájaros, dioses tutelares
y demonios menores o insulares
se afronten en tu copa. Simetría

de las robustas ramas por el suelo
imantadas, del tronco que parece
escuchar en las hojas, cuando crece

el amigo rumor. En el desvelo
vigilas tú para que el día empiece.
O para unir la tierra con el cielo.

For the Tree of "La Recoleta"

A lesson for mankind: reach out
to all the senses! In the wind
your branches are argument and emblem
of plenitude. Or banners

of supplication. The day does not begin
without birds, tutelary gods
and minor or insular demons
offending each other in your canopy. Symmetry

of robust branches over the earth
magnetized, coming from the trunk that seems
to listen to the leaves when the friendly

murmur grows. In sleepless nights
you keep vigil so that day might begin.
Or to tie the earth to the heavens.

Ornitomancia

El vuelo de los pájaros enseña
el torvo porvenir que nos espera:
su tiempo de salitre, ventolera
ululando su aciago santo y seña.

Triste, la leche aguada que no preña;
el cáncer que envenena y prolifera
burdo y taimado como la ceguera;
la que va desdentada, la sin greña.

Presentada con sorna desparpajo,
se adentró lacerando y con trabajo,
el puño preso y retorcido el brazo.

La vértebra ya cede y resquebraja,
despojada la piel de su mortaja:
tu soplo helado sobre el espinazo.

Ornithomancy

The birds' flight foretells
a cruel future that awaits us:
days of saltpeter, a wind gust
howling its tragic saint and sign.

Sad, the watery milk that won't impregnate;
a cancer that poisons and spreads
coarse and sly as blindness;
he who goes toothless, he who goes bald.

Presented with sarcasm and chaos,
he entered cutting and working,
cuffing the fist, twisting the arm.

The vertebra now gives in and cracks,
skin is stripped of its shroud:
your cold breath down my spine.

Lo que la noche le cuenta al día,
lo que el veneno le da al sediento:
la brusca saciedad de un alimento,
del licor, atenuada su alegría.

Terca voracidad del pensamiento
que acecha la aserción y la aporía.
O la verdad, opaca geometría
despojada, sin borde ni cimiento.

Un relato nocturno sin derroche
barroco. Nitidez: en cada verso
un espejo tenaz del universo,

sin amargura, elogio ni reproche.
El día no es el otro ni el reverso,
sino el centro invisible de la noche.

What night says to day,
what poison gives the parched man:
sudden plenitude of food,
of liquor, dimming his joy.

Dogged greed for thought
that creeps up on argument and deadlock.
Or truth, opaque and dispossessed
geometry, borderless, baseless.

Nocturne without baroque
waste. Clarity: in each verse
a tenacious mirror of the universe,

without grief, praise or reproach.
Day is not the other or its reverse,
but out of sight, center of night.

A Mario Bencomo

El rojo se volcó sobre el morado
y sobre el rojo un garabato obscuro,
quemada geometría sobre el muro:
ventana de otra luz y de otro lado.

La furia del brochazo enemistado:
madre del vino, púrpura clausura,
sangre rupestre sobre el agua dura,
umbral incandescente sepultado.

Aunque nunca se evoque ni se vea
el mar está presente, y la resaca
con su vitral mojado verde albahaca.

Al fondo del rectángulo espejea
un instante, si irisa, ya se opaca
el golpetazo azul de la marea.

To Mario Bencomo

Red spilled over purple
and over red a dark scribble,
burnt geometry on the wall:
window of another light from another side.

Fury of the enemy brushstroke:
mother of wine, cloistered cardinal purple,
stone blood over the hard water,
incandescent buried threshold.

Though never evoked and never seen,
the sea is present, and the undertow,
with its wet stained glass, its green basil.

In the rectangle's depths, the tide's hard blue
billowing gleams for an instant, becoming
iridescent, already darkening.

Matta dibuja lo invisible: el viento,
la dimensión de lo desconocido,
lo que no captará ningún sentido,
ni tiene forma, ni conocimiento.

El golpe de lo inmóvil. El reverso.
La fijeza del sueño y del olvido.
La transparencia gris. El estallido
de una luz fósil: la del universo.

La curva del espacio. Hélice rota
de una galaxia que se apaga: emblema
del retorno al origen que desata

la energía más densa y más remota.
Incandescencia que se expande y quema
el universo que dibuja a Matta.

Matta draws the invisible: wind,
dimensions of the unknown,
which no sense, no form,
or knowledge might capture.

The jolt of the immobile. Its reverse.
The fixity of dream and oblivion.
Gray transparency. The shatter
of fossilized light: that of the universe.

The curve of space. Broken helix
of a fading galaxy: emblem
of a return to a beginning, letting loose

the densest and most remote energy.
Incandescence expanding and burning
the universe drawing Matta.

Acróstico traidor: no restituyes
una presencia plena y sosegada,
rezagada en Berlín, o en esa nada
escueta pero cierta, de que huyes.

Lenta locura donde a veces fluyes:
inventas una torre abandonada
o la ves desde lo alto y la atribuyes,
ya que no los delirios, la mirada

sin mirada de Hölderlin. Inerte
espejismo de un río que no cesa:
verte apenas. Más bien: apenas verte.

Es cierto que intimida la belleza,
reverso del hastío y la fijeza,
o de la luz certera de la muerte.

Acrostic traitor: you don't restore
undisturbed and replete presence:
rambling behind in Berlin or in that simple,
even certain nothingness from which you flee.

Lead-footed madness where you sometimes flow:
inventing an abandoned tower
or seeing it from above and granting it,
you, no delusions, the face without a face

showing Hölderlin. Inert
endless illusion of a river without end:
viewing you barely. Better said: barely viewing you.

Exactly—beauty intimidates,
reversal of weariness and fixity,
or of the deft light of death.

Que se quede el infinito sin estrellas

A González-Esteva

Que se quede el infinito sin estrellas,
que la curva del tiempo se enderece
y pierda su fulgor, cuando se mece
un planeta en su abismo y en las huellas

del estallido primordial. Aquellas
noticias recibidas del comienzo
de las galaxias, del vacío inmenso,
hoy son luz fósil. Paradojas bellas

que anuncian por venir lo transcurrido
y postulan pasado lo futuro.
Universo del pensamiento puro:

un espacio que fluye como un río
y un tiempo sin presente, opaco y frío.
El tiempo de la espera y del olvido.

May the Infinite Be Starless

To González-Esteva

May the infinite be starless.
May the curve of time straighten
and lose its luminescence when a planet
sways in its abyss and in the remnants

of the primordial explosion. News
received from the galaxies'
beginnings, from the vast vacuum,
is today fossilized light. Pretty paradoxes

announce what's passed upon their coming
and postulate posthumously what's to come.
Universe of pure thought:

a space that flows like a river
and a time without present, opaque and cold.
The time of waiting and forgetting.

A José Triana

Le pusiste a Medea una falda de encaje.
De Flora enderezaste en tacón jorobado.
No hay rima de tu verso que no rompa y no raje,
ni estrofa en que no vuele un zunzún azorado.

La distancia no existe. Abres una ventana,
albergue de palomas huidizas, y en la nieve,
serenas aparecen por un instante breve
bajo un cielo morado las calles de La Habana.

Un cortador de caña, de Servando Cabrera,
moreno de ojos verdes y mirada de trigo,
nos custodia en París. Desde el poniente rojo

llega un olor dulzón de guarapera.
Ay Triana, no te asombres si digo
que el mulato del cuadro nos ha guiñado el ojo.

To José Triana

You put a lace skirt on Medea.
You had Flora stand tall in her hunchback heels.
There's no rhyme in your poems that doesn't break and cut,
no stanza where a stunned hummingbird doesn't fly.

Distance doesn't exist. You open a window,
shelter for the elusive dove, and in the snow,
the streets appear for a brief moment beneath
Havana's purple heavens to be serene.

A cane cutter, Servando Cabrera's,
brown with green eyes and a gaze of grain,
watches over us in Paris. From the red setting sun

arrives a sweet smell of cane juice.
Oh, Triana, don't be surprised if I tell you
the mulatto on the canvas winked at us.

A la casa de los Condes de Jaruco

Para Manuel Díaz Martínez

La casa de los Condes de Jaruco,
testigo de esplendores coloniales
empañados, duplica en sus vitrales
las curvas de la piedra y del estuco.

Con vastas espirales el bejuco
ha cubierto columnas, capiteles,
hojas de acanto, rígidos laureles
y blasones de un oro ya caduco.

No invoques a los dioses cejijuntos
para que alcen burlones sus caretas
y aparezcan de nuevo los conjuntos

habaneros. Llorando en sus macetas
las arecas están; los mediopuntos
apagan su reflejo en las losetas.

To the Home of the Counts of Jaruco

For Manuel Díaz Martínez

The home of the Counts of Jaruco,
witness of tarnished colonial splendors,
duplicates in its stained glass
curves of stone and stucco.

Vast spirals of reeds have covered
columns, their capitals, leaves
of acanthus, rigid laurels,
and blazons of gold already outdated.

Do not call on your unibrowed gods
to raise burlesque masks
and conjure again your Havana

bands. Weeping in their flowerpots
are the betel palms; the fanlights
erase their reflection on the tiles.

Recuento

Ya no soy el de ayer, el tiempo pasa.
Mi verso se ha tornado transparente.
Por las tardes me vienen de repente
bruscos deseos de volver a casa.

La pasión que ensimisma y la que abrasa
se alejaron de mí; ahora en la mente
quien disfruta, nocturna indiferente,
con los cuerpos que el día me rechaza.

No deploro el amor, que me fue ajeno;
sino el deseo, que redime, invierte
y modifica todo lo que toca.

Escrituras, pasiones y veneno
faltaron a mi vida y a mi muerte.
Y el roce de unas manos, y una boca.

Recounting

I'm no longer the man I was, time passes.
My poems have turned transparent.
In the afternoons, the sudden longing
to go home comes to me.

Consuming passion, passion that burns,
has left me; now it's my mind
that delights, indifferent night,
in those bodies that day turns away.

I do not deplore love, which was foreign to me;
only desire, which redeems, inverts,
and alters all that it touches.

Writings, passions, and poison
were missing in my life and my death.
And the touch of some hands, and a mouth.

Retrato

A los veinte años del mayo del 68

El óleo abandonó por Liquitex,
Lacan y Lévi-Strauss por Asterix;
vendió el Max Ernst y compró Otto Dix;
el amor renegó por "sea-sun-sex".

Botó el "Heno de Pravia" y usó Ajax;
dejó la Leica por la Rollyflex.
No se arriesgaba sino con Durex
y en ciudades remotas—Aix o Dax.

Su alimento era el whisky. Y el Viandox.
Se burló de Pierre Daix y de Pierre Dux
y sobre el sexo se tatuó "DE LUX".

Hoy, su *furbizia* en Wall Street es vox
populi. Y sus arreglos con el tax.
De aquellos tiempos conservó el Madrax.

Portrait

20 years after May, 1968

He abandoned oil for Liquitex,
Lacan and Lévi-Strauss for Asterix;
sold the Max Ernst and bought an Otto Dix;
blew off love for "sea-sun-sex."

He trashed "Heno de Pravia" and used Ajax;
gave up Leica for Rolleiflex.
Didn't risk it without Durex
and in remote cities—Aix or Dax.

His sustenance was whisky. And Viandox.
He messed around with Pierre Daix and Pierre Dux
and on his sex tattooed "DE LUX."

Today, his *furbizia* on Wall Street is *vox populi*. And his dealings done with tax.
From those times he saved Mandrax.

Para Héctor Bianciotti

Más que el sueño la justeza
de los rostros dibujados.
Paisajes, muros rosados.
De un pájaro la fijeza.

Todo convoca su ausencia,
reverso de los sentidos;
queda una voz, los sonidos
que la muerte no silencia.

Siguen su trazo constante
y su vasta alegoría
el ajedrez y el invierno.

Una frase en el cuaderno,
la opacidad del diamante:
lo que la noche da al día.

For Héctor Bianciotti

More than the dream, the accuracy
of drawn faces.
Landscapes, pink walls.
Of a bird, the fixity.

Everything recalls his absence,
opposing the senses;
there remains a voice, the sounds
that death does not silence.

Chess and winter follow
his vast allegory
and the constant stroke of his pen.

A phrase in his notebook,
the opacity of the diamond:
what night gives day.

DÉCIMAS

DÉCIMAS

Corona de las frutas

I. Anón

¿Quién no ha probado un anón
a la sombre de un ateje?
Danae teje y desteje
el tiempo de oro y de ron.
Empalagoso y dulzón
para el gusto no avezado;
ni verde ni apolimado
el paladar lo disfruta.
Fruta no: pulpa de fruta.
Goce: mas goce al cuadrado.

II. Mango

Se formó el arroz con mango,
rey de la gastronomía;
si hilachas de oro, armonía
tenebrosa y cruel: de tango.
Manjar del más alto rango,
heráldica de lo poco.
Aguardiente, agua de coco:
las bebidas que reclama.
¡Qué cenit—diría Lezama—,
qué corona del barroco!

A Crown of Fruits

I. Cherimoya

Who hasn't tried a cherimoya
in the shade of a Red Manjack tree?
Danaë weaves and undoes
time in gold and rum.
Sickly-sweet and sugary
for the inexperienced tongue;
neither green nor ripe
the palate takes delight.
Fruit, no: pulp of the fruit.
Pleasure: but pleasure multiplied.

II. Mango

Rice was made with mango,
king of gastronomy;
with loose threads of gold, bleak
and cruel harmony: the tango.
Feast of the highest standing,
heraldry of the few.
Aguardiente, water of the coco-
nut: the drinks he needs.
My heavens—Lezama would say—
a crown for the baroque!

III. Caimito

Por la hoja del caimito
van dos colores trepando:
blanco y verde. No sé cuándo
ni dónde nació este mito.
Salta el sinsonte contrito
y se reposa en la aldaba
de ese cenit, donde alaba
un azul más que celeste.
Y declama el sol: ¡Con éste
se acabo lo que se daba!

IV. Piña

Puse una piña pelona
sobre tres naranjas chinas,
y le añadí en las esquinas
la guayaba sabrosona.
Así, en exilio, corona
la reina insular, barroca,
la naturaleza—poca—
y muerte que le he ofrecido.
Y el emblema que la evoca:
"No habrá más penas ni olvido."

III. Star Apple

Through the leaf of the star apple
go two colors climbing:
white and green. I don't know when
or where this myth was born.
The penitent mockingbird leaps
and settles on the latch
of those heavens, where it praises
a blue beyond celestial.
And the sun proclaims: this ends
what had been given!

IV. Pineapple

I placed a bald pineapple
on three Chinese oranges,
and added in the corners
the sweetest guava.
In this way, in exile, the insular
queen crowns, baroque,
her still life—little—
and death which I've offered her.
And the emblem that it evokes:
"There will be no more pain or oblivion."

V. Papaya

Qué bien hiciste, Ramón,
en pintar una papaya,
de ese color y esa talla,
con técnica perfección.
Tu gesto es de tradición:
Heredia se volvió loco
y vio una mata de coco
en el Niágara brumoso.
Más al norte y más sabroso,
¡tú coronaste el barroco!

VI. Marañón

Si bien aprieta la boca
el marañón sabrosón,
ácido y luego dulzón
al paladar se trastoca.
Importancia tiene poca
si su jugo se derrama:
un súbito, un vago drama,
un ligero sobresalto,
cuando su rojo es más alto
que el colibrí, que la llama.

V. Papaya

Well done, Ramón,
in paining the papaya,
that color and shape,
with technical perfection.
Your gesture derives from tradition:
Heredia went loco
and saw a jungle of coco
in funny Niagara.
Farther north and more delicious,
you crowned the *barroco*!

VI. Cashew

However you close the mouth
the tasty cashew,
acidic and then sweet,
turns your palate upside down.
If you spill its juice
is of little matter:
a sudden, idle drama,
a light fright,
when its red hangs higher
than the hummingbird, than fire.

VII. Níspero

Níspero de ocre tranquilo
blasón de la piel mulata:
son que se ata y se desata
sobre una guitarra de hilo.
Noche que muere en el filo
de la luz que va brotando,
palmera garabateando
su penacho por el cielo;
níspero: gula y desvelo
de gallo que está cantando.

VIII. Guanábana

La guanábana ameniza
cualquier merienda casera:
se coge la pulpa entera
y en hielo se pulveriza;
con un terrón se eterniza
esa nevada corola
que decanta por sí sola
tan copioso frenesí.
Blanco sobre blanco. Sí:
alquimia de la champola.

VII. Loquat

Loquat of serene ochre
blazon of mulatto skin:
sound that's bound and unbound
over an acoustic guitar.
Night that dies on the edge
of budding light,
palm tree scrawling
its plume through the sky;
loquat: gluttony and sleeplessness
of the rooster singing.

VIII. Guanábana

The guanábana rouses
any homemade snack:
grab its full pulp
and pulverize in ice;
it becomes eternal
with a clod of sugar, snowy corolla,
decanting on its own
a copious frenzy.
White over white. Yes: alchemy
of *champola*: the guanábana drink.

IX. Mameya

Recuerdo el salón sombrío
y la estricta compotera,
la reja, la enredadera
y las mañanas de frío;
más que el silencio el hastío
del aciago Camagüey,
siempre añorando su grey
como un río su afluente.
Y recuerdo aún más la fuente
donde tronaba el mamey.

X. Colofón

Se acabó lo que se daba
—que era nada—y es por eso
que la carencia en exceso
también sobra. Confrontada
con su rival, la Materia,
la Nada se puso seria
y la desafió—en allegro—:
"El viento—mas no las flores—
píntamelo de colores,
o gris con pespunte negro."

IX. Mamey

I remember the dismal salon
and the strict dessert,
the bars, vines,
and cold mornings;
more than silence, the weariness
of hapless Camagüey,
always longing for its flock
as a river for its tributary.
And I remember even more the spring
where the mamey resounded.

X. Colophon

Then ended what had been given
—which was nothing—and therefore
absence in excess
is also left remaining. Confronted
with her rival, Matter,
Nothing became serious
and challenged her—in allegro—
"Wind—but not flowers—
paint it for me in colors,
or in gray with black stitches."

EN EL ÁMBAR DEL ESTÍO

A Jorge y Miguel Barnet, a LOS ORISHAS EN CUBA, *de Natalia Bolívar Aróstegui, y, claro está, a Lydia Cabrera y Pierre Fatumbi Verger*

Orishas

I. Olofi, Olordumare, Olorun

Al principio: la conciencia
ilimitada y ardiente
de Olofi, fábula y fuente
de toda posible ciencia.
Del universo la esencia
va a surgir. O surgió dentro
de un tiempo sin tiempo. Encuentro
de opuestos. Aunque distante
la llamarada es cegante
del Sol. Un ojo en el centro.

II. Elegguá

Ni comienzos hay, ni fines,
sin él, pues yace y vigila
tras la puerta, donde oscila
un trompo de colorines.
Frecuenta ron y festines;
guardián, mensajero, guía.
Va de jarana en porfía.
Si alguien silba, se enfurece.
De regalo se le ofrece
un ratón. O una jutía.

IN SUMMER'S AMBER

To Jorge and Miguel Barnet, to THE ORISHAS IN CUBA, *by Natalia Bolívar Aróstegui, and, of course, to Lydia Cabrera and Pierre Fatumbi Verger*

Orishas

I. Olofi, Olodumare, Olorun

In the beginning: consciousness
unlimited and burning
of Olofi, fable and font
of all possible science.
From the universe, his essence
will spring. Or sprang within
a time without time. The meeting
of opposites. Although distant
the Sun's flushing red
is blinding. An eye in the center.

II. Elegua

There are no beginnings, no endings
without him, as he waits and watches
behind the door, where a spinning
top of goldfinches turns.
He frequents rum and feasts;
guardian, messenger, guide.
He goes to parties with persistence.
If one whistles, he's furious.
As a gift, he's given
a mouse. Or a hutia.

III. Obatalá

Ropa blanca si le rezas.
Dieciséis plumas de loro.
Majá, marfil —y nunca oro—
al dueño de las cabezas.
Con su bastón te enderezas.
Cuida de que no se vengue
si ve juerga, orgía o jelengue.
Cascarilla, algodón, nata,
dale con grajeas de plata
y una torre de merengue.

IV. Changó

Un hacha como sombrero,
rojo y blanco, blanco y rojo;
nada apacigua el enojo
del amo, jefe, y guerrero.
Dando vueltas al carnero
se aproxima a los tambores
entre manzanas y flores.
Un rayo de luz quebrada
sobre el castillo y la espada.
Cabio Osile cuando le ores.

III. Obatala

White clothing if you pray to him.
Sixteen parrot feathers.
Boa, ivory—and never gold—
for the lord of heads.
With his cane, you stand up.
Take care he does not take revenge
if he sees revelry, orgy, or party.
Give him white *cascarilla*, cotton, cream,
with birdshots of silver
and a tower of meringue.

IV. Shango

A hatchet for a hat,
red and white, white and red;
nothing pacifies the master,
leader, warrior's wrath.
Going circles around the ram
he approaches the drummers
among apples and flowers.
A ray of light fractured
over sword and castle.
Call him *Kabiosile* when in prayer.

V. Ochún

Aparece junto al río:
rumor de pulseras de oro.
Un venado cruza el coro
en el ámbar del estío.
¡Espejos para el hastío!
De la miel, la brilladera.
Girasol en la sopera.
Mulata de rompe y raja,
el sándalo la agasaja.
—Lo dice Lydia Cabera—.

VI. Los Ibeyis

De dos en dos van las aguas
iguales y diferentes;
con sonajas estridentes,
los juguetones jimaguas.
En casa de guano y yaguas,
con sus dimes y diretes,
arman no un brete, dos bretes,
si escuchan una guitarra.
Cuando un cordel los amarra
sentados en taburetes.

V. Oshun

She appears beside the river:
rumor of golden bracelets.
A deer crosses her choir
in summer's amber.
Mirrors for her tedium!
From honey, her radiance.
Sunflower in the soup dish.
Mulatta of spirit and pleasure,
the sandalwood entertains her.
—so says Lydia Cabrera—.

VI. The Ibejis

Two in two go the waters
identical and different;
our playful twins
with raucous rattles.
In the house of balsa and royal palms,
with their chits and their chats
they fix not one, but two tricks,
if they hear a guitar.
When one chord ties them
to the stools they sit on.

VII. Oyá

Monte oscuro, noche oscura;
centellas y dos espadas.
¡Deje sus puertas cerradas
la fúnebre arquitectura!
Su paso, que se apresura,
y el mármol barroco y serio,
sellarán todo misterio.
Guarda, tras nueve colores,
guadañas, cirios y flores,
la dueña del cementerio.

VIII. Babalú Ayé

Tela zurcida y oscura.
Vendas. Llagas purulentas
que sudan sobre las cuentas
del collar que las sutura.
Ni otra forma ni más pura
del cuerpo que se quebranta.
Vino para la garganta
y dos perritos de hierro
—blanco y manchado es su perro—.
San Lázaro te levanta.

VII. Oya

Dark hill, dark night;
lightning and two swords.
Keep your doors locked,
funereal architect!
Her step, which she hastens,
and the baroque and serious marble
will seal all mystery.
She holds, behind nine colors,
scythes, altar candles and flowers,
the proprietor of the cemetery.

VIII. Babalú-Ayé

Dark fabric with seams.
Bandages. Festering ulcers
sweating over the beads
of the necklace that sutures them.
There is no purer bodily form
that breaks down.
Wine for the throat
and two little iron dogs
—his is spotted and white—.
Saint Lazarus wakes you up.

IX. Olokun

Mitad hombre, mitad pez,
yace con siete cadenas
más allá de las arenas.
En sueño lo vi una vez:
del rostro la redondez
con hondas rayas tribales
y ojos blancos abisales
ahuyenta ese mal severo.
Boca abajo, en el tablero,
dieciséis *cauris* rituales.

X. Yemayá

Madre de agua, Luna nueva:
una paloma, un cordero,
ofreceré al mar austero,
para pasar esta prueba.
La vida muerte conlleva.
Una cruz de cascarilla
sobre la frente amarilla:
firmarás mi último aliento.
Y contra marea y viento
remaré. Hasta la otra orilla...

IX. Olokun

Half man, half fish,
he lies with seven chains
beyond the beaches.
I saw him once in sleep:
the roundness of his face,
with deep tribal lines
and white abysmal eyes,
dispels that *mal severo*.
Face down, on the table,
sixteen ritual cowrie shells.

X. Yemoja

Mother of water, new Moon:
a dove, a lamb,
I will offer to the austere sea,
that I might pass this test.
With life comes death.
A cross of white *cascarilla*
over the yellow forehead:
you will write my final breath.
And against tide and wind
I'll row. Until I reach the other shore…

OTRAS DÉCIMAS

A partir de frases dichas en español por F.W.

De tu cuerpo en el jardín
vino a bañarse el coquí
sediento, y econtró allí
frescura. Puede que al fin
después de tanto trajín
en su safrán de azafrán
haya logrado su afán,
y con la tarde lunada
fijado canto y morada
en cielo de celofán.

OTHER DÉCIMAS

From Phrases Spoken in Spanish by F.W.

From your body in the garden
the thirsty coquí came to bathe
and then it cooled down. Possibly, in the end
after so much hustle
for saffron from crocuses
he whet his desire,
and in the lunar afternoon
found his home and song
in the skies of cellophane.

Convenzo más cuando engaño,
soy más credible si miento
—simulado sentimiento
si persuade, no hace daño—.
Así transcurro, y el año
torna menos largo y cruento
si el afuera es un adentro
y el adentro es un afuera.
Más fingiría si no fuera
que aparentar aparento.

I convince the more I deceive;
I'm more believed if I lie
—simulated sentiment,
if persuasive, doesn't leave injury—.
That's how I get by, and the year
grows less bloody and long
if what's out is what's in
and what's in is what's out.
I'd feign being more
if seeming to be I did not seem.

A Juan Goytisolo

Tal eres, tiempo de duelo,
que todo ayer fue una fiesta:
cuando el ángel de la siesta
retozaba por el suelo.
Aliabierto, fijo en vuelo,
equilibrado y clemente,
planeaba sobre el durmiente
el pájaro solitario
de plumas abecedario.
Faltó el aire de repente.

To Juan Goytisolo

This is what you are, time of grieving,
all yesterday a fiesta
when the angel of sleeping
gambolled on the ground.
Open-winged, fixed in flight,
balanced and merciful,
the solitary bird
of abecedarian feathers
soared above the sleeper.
Then the air went missing.

ÚLTIMOS POEMAS

(1999)

LAST POEMS

(1999)

UNO

ONE

Enemigo rostro idéntico,
ángel saltón, libro lacio
hojea ojo de batracio
vociferando su idéntico

jaguar gótico. No reza
ni recompone las aves
de azufre, las flautas suaves
de dios sin pies ni cabeza.

Espejo cóncavo río
que arrastra máquinas, vuelo
de tigre al revés. El hielo

circular oye el estío
de la presencia: potente
enemigo, rostro yente.

s.f.

Enemy identical face,
vibrant angel, wilted book
leafed through with batrachian eye
boasting about its identical

gothic jaguar. He does not pray
or mend the birds
of sulfur, the soft flutes
of the gods without feet or head.

Concave river mirror
that carries machines, flight
of tiger upside down. The circular

ice hears the summer
of presence: potent
enemy, fleeting face.

n.d.

El oro de *El Conde Orgaz*
el rosa viejo y el gris
de Morandi, o el matiz
apenas visible tras

el color, que es un disfraz
o un simulacro feliz
del no-color: "la raíz
del *blanco*" (en Octavio Paz).

En Bonnard, otra embriaguez:
el naranja, que va en pos
del fuego oculto en la luz.

No la luz; la lucidez
de Rothko: antes de la cruz,
ese era el rostro de Dios.

s.f.

The gold in *The Count of Orgaz,*
Morandi's gray and old rose,
or the shade that's
hard to glimpse

behind the color, a disguise
or the no-color's
happy simulacrum: "the white's
root" (from Octavio Paz).

In Bonnard, another drunkenness:
the orange, that hides
behind the blaze

in light. In light, no; the lucidity
of Rothko: before the cross
that was God's face.

n.d.

Imitación de un soneto de Miguel de Guevara (¿1585–1646?) y de dos de Ulalume González de León
El tiempo y la cuenta

La vida se acabó. No me di cuenta
de la velocidad que lleva el tiempo
en su opaco fluir, ni de que cuenta
cada instante perdido. Tiempo al tiempo

se fueron—antes de sacar la cuenta—
los años en los días, como el tiempo
de arena, que parece que no cuenta
cada grano: un átomo de tiempo

que nada recupera. Date cuenta
de cómo entre las manos se va el tiempo
sacando, en un soneto, austera cuenta.

No me reproches que no tienes tiempo
si en total faltó lo que más cuenta:
la obscura enemistad del Ser y el Tiempo.

1986

Imitation of a Sonnet by Miguel de Guevara (1585-1646?) and of two by Ulalume González de León
Time and the Count

Life has ended. I didn't take into account
the pace that carried time
in its opaque flow, or see that it counts
every instant as lost. From time to time

they went—before being accounted
for—the years in the days, how time's
hourglass, seemingly does not count
each grain of sand: each atom of time

which nothing recovers. Recount
how, between the hands, time
goes taking, in a sonnet, austere account.

Don't blame me for not having time
if, all in all, you're missing what most counts:
that obscure enemy of Being and Time.

1986

Sin más demora le pedí la cuenta
con el pretexto de que se iba el tiempo
y no alcanzaba lo único que cuenta,
lo que por un instante anula el tiempo.

A subterfugios acudió sin cuenta,
para que ese anodino pasatiempo
alcanzara su fin, a fin de cuenta.
Pero todo era torpe, o a destiempo.

No sé qué sucedió. No me di cuenta
de que ya había pasado tanto tiempo
en aquel juego de siniestra cuenta

en que todo fue hastío y contratiempo,
queriendo enderezar a riesgo y cuenta
hasta la curva del espacio-tiempo.

1986

With no further delay I asked for the bill, counting
on the excuse: *I'm running out of time,*
I might not make the single thing that counts,
which for a moment blots out time.

He resorted to a subterfuge there's no accounting
for, so that the anodyne pastime
might come to an end, by all accounts.
But all was blundered, or badly timed.

I don't know what happened. I didn't account
for the fact that already so much time
had passed in that play of sinister counter

games, where all was boredom, set against time,
wanting, as I did, to rectify the risk and count,
even the curve of space and time.

1986

A las letras del alfabeto

Ardiente letra, tu sangre será
breve, como las flores del baobab.
Crearás palabras, y otras letras (*sic*)
de éstas caerán, en un torpe ardid.

En otro reino la escritura fue
fragmento, cuña, nudo, raga y kif;
grave estampido de un dorado gong,
huella y espejo de un antiguo aleph:
imagen que el espacio da de sí.

Juntan las letras al sol y al reloj,
—Kafka se encuentra con su doble, K:
lenta escritura de un rumor letal—,
llenan, combinan, como dijo Lull.
Mallarmé no lo olvida, ni el Islam,
ni el monje que enseñó bajo el monzón,
o el que con letras escribió y oró.

Piet Mondrian pinta escuchando be-bop.
¿Quién es Duchamp y quién HOOQ?
¿Refléjase en lo nimio y lo estelar
—signos, silencios—no la sombra, más
todo el ser de la luz, como en Rembrandt?
Universo de letras donde tú
ves ciudades pintadas: Tel-aviv,
Westminster por Monet, la gris Glasgow;
xilografía de la tosca Sfax.

Y aquí la firma: Severo Sarduy
—zurdo algoritmo de la tozudez—.

Ginebra, 8-8-88

To the Letters of the Alphabet

Ardent letter, your blood will be ephemera,
brief, like flowers of the baobab,
creating words that other leters (*sic*)
drop from, a ruse, blundered.

Elsewhere, writing was in another empire
fragment, crib, knot, raga, and kif;
grave thunder of a golden gong,
hint and reflection of an ancient aleph:
image that the space gives of its own *I*.

Joining together letters, sun, and haj,
—Kafka finds himself with his double, K:
lackadaisical writing of a rumor that's lethal—,
llano filled, combined, in the words of Lull.
Mallarmé doesn't forget this, nor does Islam,
nor the monk who taught in the monsoon,
or he who wrote with letters and prayed, oh

Piet Mondrian paints listening to be-bop.
Question: who is Duchamp and who HOOQ?
Reflected in the trivial and the stellar
—signs, silences—do we not see the shadow? Or is
there indeed all the being of light, as in Rembrandt?
Universe of letters where you
view painted cities: Tel-Aviv,
Westminster by Monet, the gray Glasgow;
xylography of the crude Sfax.

Yet, here is his signature: Severo Sarduy—
zagging, left-handed algorithm of stubborn glitz—.

Geneva, 8-8-88

Notes

"A las letras del alfabeto" es un doble ABC. Cada verso comienza y termina con una letra del alfabeto, siguiendo el orden. El simple ABC es un género tradicional de la literatura brasilera: Castro Alves lo practicó con frecuencia y, entre los contemporáneos, Jorge Amado lo ha recuperado, en prosa. Dedica una novela a Castro Alves siguiendo el procedimiento, las letras son asimiladas a capítulos. Añadí pues, al ABC brasilero la norma de utilizar la misma letra al final de cada verso.

C.—El *sic* señala una tautología: las letras crearán palabras que a su vez crean letras.

F.—Cuatro sistemas de notación escriptural: lo fragmentario, lo cuneiforme, el nudo precortesiano, la reciente voga india; raga y kif.

LL.—El arte combinatorio, de Lull, como imagen textual del universo, que volverá a evocar Mallamré.

P.—Mondrian pinta *Fox-trot* en 1927. Sus últimos cuadros son *Trafalgar Square* y *Broadway Boogie-Woogie* de 1944. No me parece abusivo incluir en la serie al *Be-bop*.

Q.—En 1919 Duchamp orna el retrato de la Gioconda con unos bigotes y la inscripción LHOOQ, fonéticamente "tiene calor en el culo". Pongo en paralelo las rupturas, igualmente subversivas, aunque de signo contrario, de Mondrian y de Duchamp, como gestos desacralizadores del arte en el siglo XX. Las otras letras no requieren mayor elucidación. [S.S.]

Notes

"To the Letter of the Alphabet" is a double abecedarian. Every line begins and ends with a letter of the alphabet, following each other in order. The simple abecedarian is a traditional genre in Brazilian literature: Castro Alves used it frequently and, among contemporaries, Jorge Amado has recuperated it in prose. He dedicates a novel to Castro Alves following the procedure, the letters are assimilated to chapters. To the Brazilian abecedarian I then added the rule of using the same letter at the end of each line.

C.—*Sic* signals a tautology: letters will create words that in turn create letters.

F.—Four systems of scriptural notation: fragmentary, cuneiform, the pre-Cortesian knot, the recent Indian fad; raga and kif.

LL.—The combinatorial art, of Lull, as textual image of the universe, which will return to evoke Mallarmé.

P.—Mondrian paints *Fox Trot* in 1927. His last paintings are *Trafalgar Square* and *Broadway Boogie-Woogie* from 1944. I do not think it's abusive to include *Be-bop* in the series.

Q.—In 1919 Duchamp adorns the Mona Lisa with a moustache and the inscription LHOOQ, phonetically "she is hot in the ass." I place these ruptures in parallel form, equally subversive, although in opposite order, Mondrian and Duchamp, as art's desacralizing gestures in the 20th century. The other letters do not require further explanation. [S.S.]

DOS

TWO

Imitación

> En la interior bodega
> de mi Amado bebí, y cuando salía
> por toda aquesta bega
> ya cosa no sabía
> y el ganado perdí que antes seguía.
>
> > San Juan de la Cruz,
> > *Cántico espiritual*, 26

Médula que florece,
hueso que goza de la torpe mano
y así menos padece
del cuerpo tan cercano
que solicita y que suplica en vano.

Si otorgar decidiste
lo que tanto mi sed encarecía,
con tal maña lo hiciste
que apenas si sabía:
cerveza trabajaba en mí fluía.

Logrado su disfrute,
aceza el deseoso y desfallece;
que un testigo lo escrute
si otro lo compadece
cuando finge que añora y que perece.

Bálsamo no reclamo,
ni alcohol que me sosiegue y restituya
el sello de lo que amo.
En todo lo que fluya
acecho quedará y presencia tuya.

(continued)

Imitation

> I drank in the inner depths
> of my Beloved's winery, and while I left
> walking through the meadow
> I knew nothing
> and I had lost the flock, which before I followed.
>
> Saint John of the Cross
Spiritual Canticle, 26

Marrow that blooms,
bone that enjoys the clumsy hand
and in this way suffers
the body less, so close,
beseeching and begging for it in vain.

If you chose to reward
my thirst with what it craves,
then you did so with such skill
that I hardly knew:
beer worked in me and flowed.

Reaping this pleasure,
the desirous one pants and faints;
may some witness scrutinize
another who pities him
when he feigns longing and perishes.

I do not require balms,
not alcohol which calms and restores
the stamp of what I love.
In all that flows
vigilance and your presence will remain.

(continued)

El ámbar que me baña
opaca transparencia que espejea,
no macula ni daña.
Lo que más se desea:
que el ser de su retiro escape, y sea.

En menos te deslizas
de lo que canta un gallo con premura,
y penetrando atizas
cuando el alba fulgura
lo que no cicatriza ni sutura.

Lacre rojo tu huella,
en la sangre cifrada tu escritura;
la firma que la sella,
la muerte que conjura
en tu fuerza se funda y configura.

El sol en su declive
los metales lastima y enrojece;
la curva que describe
cuando la luz decrece
en tu cuerpo se invierte y amanece.

Ya nada me intimida:
llaga ni lancinante quemadura,
ni a mi tacto convida
la tersa vestidura
porque sé que es irreal y que no dura.

Lo que viste tu pecho:
el músculo en tensión y movimiento,
y le sirve de lecho
al soplo, y de sustento
a la vida, al ritmo y al aliento.

(continued)

Amber that bathes me
opaque transparency which gleams,
neither stains nor harms.
What is most desired:
that the being of his refuge escapes, and is.

You glide more quickly
than a cock's quick crow,
and penetrating when day breaks
you stoke
that which does not scar or suture.

Let your trace be red,
your writing ciphered in blood;
signature which seals it,
death, conjured
in your force, is founded and configured.

The sun in setting
wounds and turns metals red;
when light dwindles
the arch it traces
on your body is reflected and rises.

Now nothing intimidates me:
neither blister or burning puncture,
my touch does not invite
the starched vestments
because I know they are not real and do not last.

What your chest wears:
the muscle in tension and moving,
which serves as a bed
in exhalation, and as sustenance
in life, at your rhythm and breath.

(continued)

Acude a mi desvelo,
no me prives de todo lo que añoro;
no concibo más cielo
que el cielo donde imploro
de tu cuerpo la fuerte lluvia de oro.

En sosiego vivía;
mi cuerpo de sí mismo se ha exiliado,
y gusta todavía
de aquello que, callado,
le entregaste de noche, rebosado.

Embriagaba más que el vino
el néctar que gusté de tu bodega,
ya perdí tacto y tino,
ya nada me sosiega,
sino el derrame que deslumbra y ciega.

c. 1992

Witness my sleeplessness,
do not deny me everything I long for;
I cannot conceive of more heaven
than the heaven where I beg of your body
the heavy golden shower.

I was living in peace;
my body has become exiled from itself,
and gains pleasure still
from that which, hushed,
you gave it at night, running over.

More than wine, the nectar I relished
from your cellar made me drunk,
now I've lost touch and caution,
now nothing soothes me,
but for the spill that shines and blinds.

c.1992

TRES

THREE

Epitafios

I

Yace aquí, sordo y severo
quien suelas tantas usó
y de cadera abusó
por delantero y postrero.
Parco adagio—y agorero—
para inscribir en su tumba
—la osamenta se derrumba,
oro de joyas deshechas—:
su nombre, y entre dos fechas,
"el muerto se fue de rumba."

II

Aquí reposa burlón,
ángel de la jiribilla,
el mago de la cuartilla
y hasta del más puro son.
Un trago de ron peleón,
un buen despojo, una misa
y un brindis seco y sin prisa
para aplacar a los dioses
ausentes, sino feroces:
¡Al que se murió de risa!

(continued)

Epitaphs

I

Here lies, deaf and severe,
he who used so many shoes'
soles, whose hips he abused
from the front and from behind.
Laconic adagio—and soothsayer—
inscribe on his tomb
—the skeleton crumbles,
gold of jewels undone—:
his name, and between two dates,
"the dead man's out to dance."

II

Here rests the jokester,
angel of the anxious,
magician of the page
and even the purest song.
A swig of cheap rum,
a good dispossession, a Mass
and an unrushed, dry toast
to appease the missing
yet ferocious gods:
to he who died of laughter!

(continued)

III

Volveré, pero no en vida,
que todo se despelleja
y el frío la cal aqueja
de los huesos. ¡Qué atrevida
la osamenta que convida
a su manera a danzar!
No la puedo contrariar:
la vida es un sueño fuerte
de una muerte hasta otra muerte,
y me apresto a despertar.

IV

A Rafael Rosado

Un epitafio discreto
pero burlón nos hermana
ante la nada cercana
que ya no tiene secreto
para nosotros. Decreto
de una deidad rezagada
que se vengó. Apolimada
quedarás, vuelta ceniza;
un coágulo por camisa:
muerta pero no olvidada.

(continued)

III

I will return, but not in life,
once my body is skinless
and lime afflicts the cold
in my bones. How impudent
the skeleton who invites me,
in his way, to dance!
I cannot resist him:
life is a heavy dream
from one death to another death,
and I'm ready to wake up.

IV

To Rafael Rosado

A discrete yet teasing
epitaph connects us
to our approaching nothingness
which now holds no secret
for us. Decree
of a lagging deity
who avenged himself. You will
be bruised, become ash;
a clot of blood for a shirt:
dead but not forgotten.

(continued)

V

Qué remolona eres, muerte
para asestar tu castigo
—aquí reposa un testigo—.
Asombra, y hasta divierte
verte laboriosa y verte
parca, desaparecer.
Al goce de obedecer,
a la vértebra jocosa
cerco de ceniza acosa:
ese es tu modo de ser.

VI

Feroz, como un latigazo
de podredumbre y andrajo,
el violento escupitajo
de la muerte. No hay abrazo
más fiel ni a más largo plazo.
Dos fechas como sudario
de estilo seco y sumario:
mi confesión y anatema.
Joya, colofón y emblema
de barroco funerario.

(continued)

V

Death, you are so lazy
in delivering your sentence
—here rests your witness—.
It astonishes and even delights
to see you labor, to see you
scarce, to see your disappearance
with the pleasure
of surrender, your siege of ash
hounding the funny vertebrae:
that's your way of being.

VI

Savage, like the lashing
of rags and putrefaction,
death's violent gob
of spit. There's no embrace
more faithful or long-term.
Two dates as shroud
of dry and brief design:
my confession and abomination.
Jewel, colophon, and emblem
of the baroque funeral.

(continued)

VII

Que den guayaba con queso
y haya son en mi velorio;
que el protocolo mortuorio
se acorte y limite a eso.
Ni lamentos en exceso,
ni Bach; música ligera:
La Sonora Matancera.
Para gustos, los colores:
a mí no me pongan flores
si muero en la carretera.

c. 1992

VII

At my funeral, may there be
cheese and guava and music;
may the mortuary protocols be
abridged and limited.
No excessive lamenting,
no Bach; light music:
play *La Sonora Matancera*.
For good taste, colors:
don't lay flowers on me
if, on the highway, I die.

c. 1992

Biographies

Novelist, poet, painter, and literary theorist, **Severo Sarduy** was one of the most groundbreaking Latin American writers of the twentieth century. Born in Camagüey, Cuba in 1937, he moved to Havana in 1956 to study medicine, but soon gave up his scientific pursuits for the arts. Following Fidel Castro's victory in the Cuban Revolution, Sarduy won a scholarship to study art criticism in Europe. He boarded a ship to Madrid in December of 1959 and, a gay man viewing Castro's increasingly homophobic regime from abroad, never went back to the island.

Often homoerotic and imbued with allusions to art, the absent or decaying body, the history of science, jazz and folk music, insular landscapes, and the author's Spanish, African, and Chinese heritage, Sarduy's poetry has rarely appeared in translation, but his literary oeuvre is vast and includes the landmark novel *From Cuba with a Song* (1967), translated by Suzanne Jill Levine in 1972. Sarduy's third book, *Cobra* (1971), won France's Medici Prize and high praise from Roland Barthes, who called it, "a paradisiac text... the pledge of continuous jubilation, the moment when by its very excess verbal pleasure chokes and reels into bliss." For his part, Richard Howard hailed Sarduy as a writer who "has everything... so brilliant, so funny, and so bewilderingly apt in his borrowings, his derivations, as well as in his inventions."

Sarduy was so prolific with his verbal innovations that Gabriel García Márquez once called him the best writer in the Spanish language. His neo-baroque style influenced such Spanish-language novelists as Mario Vargas Llosa, Juan Goytisolo, and Carlos Fuentes while his involvement in Parisian literary circles and work with the publishing house Editions du Seuil is responsible for bringing *One Hundred Years of Solitude* into the French language. From 1960 until the time of his death, the poet lived in Paris, where he worked with Roland Barthes, Phillipe Sollers, and Julia Kristeva, among many others, on the literary magazine *Tel Quel*. Sarduy died due to complications with AIDS in 1993.

David Francis serves as Dean of Grace Hopper College at Yale University, where he teaches in the Program in Ethnicity, Race, and Migration. He has received a Fulbright fellowship to translate into English poems by the Colombian writer José Asunción Silva. His translations or poems have appeared in *Inventory*, *The FSG Book of 20th-Century Latin American Poetry*, *Guernica*, *Exchanges*, *The Brooklyn Rail*, *The Chronicle of Higher Education*, and elsewhere. He has an M.F.A. in poetry writing from Columbia University and a Ph.D. in Romance Languages and Literatures from Harvard University. He taught previously at Tufts, Harvard, and the University of Virginia.

Circumference Books is a press for poetry in translation. Our books highlight the process of translation and how that work is rooted in collaboration. Each multi-lingual project foregrounds original design solutions, making visual the relationships between languages, cultures, writers, and translators. Circumference Books supports the creative and urgent work of bridging cultures and languages. Our projects spotlight non-national languages and foster cross-linguistic poetic exchange.

Circumference Books would not be possible without our

FOUNDING MEMBERS

Carrie Olivia Adams · Elina Alter · Samuel Amadon
Stephanie Anderson · Mary Jo Bang · Jessica Baran
Josephine Pickford Beeman · Alexandra O. Betlyon · Paul Bisagni
Patrick & Christine Brosnan · Jennifer Chang · Don Mee Choi
Hillary Cookler · Mónica de la Torre · Sharon Dolin · Danielle Dutton
Elaine Garza · Gabrielle Giattino · Eric Giroux · Sonja Greckol
Sandra Guerreiro · Rita Kronovet · Steven Kronovet
Brett Fletcher Lauer · Angie Lee · Martha Lewin & Jack Egan
E. J. McAdams · Tamerra Moeller · Michelle Gil-Montero
Trey Moody · Erín Moure · Idra Novey · Carl Phillips
James Shea & Dorothy Tse · David Shook · Stephen Sparks
Christina Svendsen · Tree Swenson · Zach Tackett
Hugh Thomas · Michael Welt · Jesse Wilbur · Jeffrey Yang

Find out more about membership:

www.circumferencebooks.com